HARNESSING MIGRATION FOR INCLUSIVE GROWTH AND DEVELOPMENT IN SOUTHERN AFRICA

SPECIAL REPORT

Jonathan Crush, Belinda Dodson, Vincent Williams, Daniel Tevera

ACKNOWLEDGEMENTS

This project was funded by UK aid from the UK government; however, the views expressed do not necessarily reflect the UK government's official policies. We would like to thank the following for their assistance with various aspects of the conceptualization, research, writing and production of this report: Fiona Clark, Bronwen Dachs, Caroline Skinner, Cathy Chames, Nana Davies, Tracey Phillips, Andries Mangokwana, Mariella Salamone and Saskia Greyling. Our thanks also to the many individuals and organizations who consented to be interviewed for this study and to Southern Hemisphere Consulting for conducting the interviews.

Published by the Southern African Migration Programme, International Migration Research Centre, Balsillie School of International Affairs, Waterloo, Ontario, Canada
http://samponline.org

First published 2017

ISBN 978-1-920596-32-3

Production by Bronwen Dachs Muller, Cape Town

Printed by Topcopy, Cape Town

TABLE OF CONTENTS

LIST OF TABLES

LIST OF FIGURES

LIST OF APPENDICES

ACRONYMS AND ABBREVIATIONS

ACMS	African Centre for Migration and Society
ACP	African Common Position on Migration and Development
AU	African Union
AUF	African Union Framework
BLS	Botswana, Lesotho and Swaziland
CESARE	Co-operation for the Enhancement of SADC Regional Economic Integration
COMESA	Common Market for Eastern and Southern Africa
CSO	Civil Society Organization
DFID	Department for International Development
DRC	Democratic Republic of the Congo
DWP	Decent Work Programme
EAC	East African Community
EU	European Union
GCRO	Gauteng City-Region Observatory
GP	Green Paper on International Migration
ICBT	Informal Cross-Border Trade
ICMPD	International Centre for Migration Policy Development
ICRMW	International Convention on the Protection of the Rights of All Migrant Workers and Members of Their Families
IDPs	Internally Displaced People
IFAD	International Fund for Agricultural Development
IFALLFD	Institute for Applied Labour Law and Farmworkers Developmental
ILO	International Labour Organization
IMRC	International Migration Research Centre
IOC	Indian Ocean Commission
IOM	International Organization for Migration
JLMP	Joint Labour Migration Programme
JPCs	Joint Permanent Commissions
LEDRIZ	Labour and Economic Development Research Institute of Zimbabwe

LHR	Lawyers for Human Rights
LMPF	Labour Migration Policy Framework
MIDSA	Migration Dialogue for Southern Africa
MiWorc	Migrating for Work Research Consortium
NGOs	Non-Governmental Organizations
NIDS	National Income Dynamics Study
ODI	Overseas Development Institute
OSISA	Open Society Initiative for Southern Africa
PASSOP	People Against Suffering, Oppression and Poverty
PF	Programming Framework
PRSPs	Poverty Reduction Strategy Plan
QLFS	Quarterly Labour Force Survey
RCPs	African Regional Consultative Processes
RISDP	Regional Indicative Strategic Development Plan
SADC	Southern African Development Community
SADSAWU	South African Domestic Service and Allied Workers Union
SAMP	Southern African Migration Programme
SAT	Southern Africa Trust
SATUC	South African Trade Union Council
SDGs	Sustainable Development Goals
SIDA	Swedish International Development Co-operation Agency
SURE	Scaling Up Remittances
TEBA	The Employment Bureau of Africa
TVET	Technical and Vocational Education and Training
UN	United Nations
UNDP	United Nations Development Programme
UNECA	United Nations Economic Commission for Africa
UNHCR	United Nations High Commissioner for Refugees
UNRISD	United Nations Research Institute for Social Development
VA	Valetta Accord
ZCTU	Zimbabwe Congress of Trade Unions

ABOUT THE AUTHORS

Dr **Jonathan Crush** is a professor and the CIGI Chair in Global Migration and Development at the Balsillie School of International Affairs (BSIA), Waterloo, Canada. He is the founder and director of the Southern African Migration Programme (SAMP) and has published extensively on issues of migration and development, diaspora engagement and food security in Africa.

Dr **Belinda Dodson** is an associate professor in the Department of Geography at Western University, London, Ontario, Canada. Her research examines the intersection of gender, migration and development, with a regional focus on Southern Africa.

Vincent Williams is a South African freelance trainer/facilitator and researcher for various institutions and organizations. He has been involved in migration policy processes in South Africa and in the region since 1997.

Dr **Daniel Tevera** is a professor in the Department of Geography at the University of the Western Cape, South Africa. His research addresses socio-spatial issues in the Global South, including urban governance, urban food security and migration.

EXECUTIVE SUMMARY

The primary goal of this study is to present the results of a comprehensive scope of key opportunities and challenges for harnessing migration for inclusive growth and development at the regional level in Southern Africa. The main objectives were as follows:

- Provide an overview of regional migration stocks and flows identifying regional trends, drivers and impacts from existing research literature and official data;

- Profile migrant characteristics at the regional level including demographic composition, types of migration and occupational profile;

- Examine the relevance of multilateral, continental and regional migration instruments, policies, protocols, agreements and forums with a view to identifying actions required to move the regional migration management agenda forward and align with the goal of enhancing migration for inclusive growth and development in Southern Africa;

- Analyze the key initiatives, opportunities and obstacles to developing a coherent, integrated and rights-regarding approach to migration management including areas of common commitment and ownership, and points of actual and potential conflict and disagreement between states;

- Conduct a gender analysis of regional migration dynamics including gender dimensions of migration, challenges, dangers and vulnerabilities confronting migrant women and other vulnerable groups, and gender analysis of migration management in Southern Africa;

- Identify potential programming areas that are weak or underdeveloped.

The report relies on data and information from four main sources: (a) existing research literature and data on regional migration dynamics and trends in Southern Africa; (b) official data sources, where available, to identify current patterns, trends and types of migration; (c) bilateral global migration data sets compiled by the UNDP and the World Bank; and (d) a programme of field research involving key informant interviews and consultations with stakeholders, international organizations and donors, national government departments, and representatives from civil society, business, labour and the academy. Country visits were undertaken to South Africa, Mozambique, Botswana and Zimbabwe. A total of 60 interviews were conducted with 86 interviewees.

The first two sections of the report outline the objectives and methodology of the research. The third section provides a contextual analysis of regional migration in Southern Africa to demonstrate that migration is a quintessentially regional issue and development challenge. There are a number of reasons why a regional – as opposed to a purely national – conceptual and policy approach to migration is desirable and necessary:

- Cross-border movements of people have a long history and constitute one of the major mechanisms of regional integration in Southern Africa (along with trade and investment). Goods and capital move relatively freely and legally across the region but people still face considerable obstacles and barriers to movement;

- Vast differences in levels of development and employment opportunities across the region have led to extremely uneven migration flows. All countries both send and receive migrants but the balance between the two varies significantly. Zimbabwe was a major destination before 2000 but has since become the region's single largest exporter of migrants. South Africa is the major destination;

- Temporary, circular migration is the norm in the region with migrants retaining close ties with home countries and communities through formal and informal transfers of cash and goods in the form of remittances. In effect, migration and remittances have become a major source of development finance across the region;

- The majority of migration movements within and to the Southern African region fall into the category of South-South migration. This form of migration, from one developing country to another, can have positive and simultaneous development impacts on both countries of origin and destination;

- From a migration management perspective, regional organizations have recognized the importance of regional harmonization and co-ordinated action. However, governments have been slower to recognize the reality of regional migration, leading to a disjuncture between initiatives to facilitate movement and co-ordinate migration for development at the continental and regional level, and national governments that tend to view migration negatively and avoid any binding commitment to regional migration processes and instruments.

The analysis of migration trends and flows distinguishes between (a) migration within the Southern African region from one country to another; (b) migration to Southern Africa from other countries, especially the rest of Africa;

and (c) migration from Southern Africa to other parts of the globe. Each has implications and opportunities for harnessing migration for development and inclusive growth. For example:

- All of the countries of Southern Africa host some migrants, with the major migration destinations being South Africa, Zimbabwe, the Democratic Republic of the Congo (DRC), Tanzania, Mozambique, Malawi and Botswana. All are also migrant-sending countries with the major intra-regional senders being Mozambique, Zimbabwe, Lesotho, Malawi and Angola. Even South Africa sends migrants to other countries in the region. In policy terms, this means that although many countries are threatened by what they view as an uncontrolled influx of migrants, they are themselves also migrant senders and beneficiaries of out-migration to other countries.

- Migration flows within the region have undergone major changes in the last two decades, including a significant decline in forced (refugee) migration, an equally significant increase in migration for economic and livelihood reasons, more diversity in flows including increasing female and youth migration, a decline in formal contract migration to South African mines, and a concomitant increase in unregulated, informalized migration across borders. Data and reliable information on all of these trends and their drivers are largely absent.

- In total, 53% of all Southern Africa-born migrants are living outside the region. The five major sending countries are South Africa, Zimbabwe, Angola, the DRC and Mauritius. The five major destinations are the United Kingdom, Australia, France, the United States and Portugal. Shared histories and common languages have resulted in the emergence of migration corridors that include South Africa-UK, South Africa-Australia, Angola-Portugal, Zimbabwe-UK and Madagascar-France. The majority of migrants who leave the region are relatively skilled, leading to claims that countries of destination are responsible for a "brain drain" from the region. This argument has largely been replaced by the realization that these migrants are actually a resource with a potentially strong development role to play.

Against the backdrop of complex and shifting migration patterns and flows, the report identifies key development-related implications of these migration trends and characteristics and presents relevant information and data on each. This provides substantive context and a link to the programming recommendations later in the report. The five areas are: (a) gender and migration; (b) migrant rights and protections; (c) migration and remittances; (d) migration and informal entrepreneurship and (e) diasporas for development. Although the available information on each area is uneven across the region, evidence is marshalled to suggest that each offers important opportunities for meeting the overall goal of harnessing migration for development and inclusive growth. These areas are united by a focus on the importance and development implications of women's migration. The major findings from the analysis of these five areas include the following:

- Southern Africa is undergoing a process of feminization of migration with increased independent women's migration. The number of female migrants in SADC is now over 2 million. In the major destination country (South Africa), the proportion of female migrants has reached 40% of the total. Gender-disaggregated data on migrant flows and occupations is generally unavailable, although South African data suggests that a migrant woman has only a 56% probability of being employed compared to a migrant man.

- There is a growing body of case-study evidence on informal temporary migration and the low wage regime and exploitative conditions in sectors such as construction, illicit mining, commercial agriculture and domestic work. For those migrant women who are employed, many are engaged in precarious livelihoods. Some are employed in potentially exploitative conditions with weak oversight or protection of their labour rights, for example as domestic or agricultural workers. Others are engaged in inherently precarious informal occupations such as trading, hair braiding and other beauty services, or craft production and sales, often conducted in unsafe spaces. Related to their precarious working and living conditions, female migrants experience gender-based violence and other health vulnerabilities.

- Poor treatment of female migrants on the way to and at the workplace exercises an extremely negative impact on the migrants themselves and their households, and is also antithetical to development and inclusive growth in their home countries. Low wages and other forms of financial extortion, for example, significantly reduce the remitting ability of migrants. Precarious employment in the agricultural and domestic service sectors is highly gendered with female migrants being most vulnerable to exploitation by formal and informal labour brokers and recruiters, employers and the authorities (especially the police).

- There is a considerable evidence that remitting is an extremely common practice in Southern Africa. However, much remitting is through informal channels, and accurate data on remittance flows at the regional level is not available. The World Bank calculates that remittance flows to the countries of Southern Africa reached USD1 billion in 2014. Only a third of remittances to Southern African countries come from other countries within the region. Over two-thirds of remittances to Southern African countries therefore come from *outside* the region.

- Globally, female migrants send approximately the same per capita amount of remittances as male migrants but women tend to send a higher proportion of their income. Women also usually send money more regularly and for longer periods of time than men. In Southern Africa there is some evidence of distinct gender differences in remitting amounts, frequency and means of remitting, remittance recipients and use of remittances. This suggests that data, research and policy-making on migration and remittances needs to be gender-disaggregated.

- The number of migrants running small and micro-enterprises or being employed by these businesses is considerable in towns and cities across the region. In South Africa, as many as one-third of migrants are self-employed in the informal economy. Surveys of migrant entrepreneurs show that the sector is dominated by young people and that women occupy particular niches. Informal business owners have positive development impacts in countries of destination and origin through remittance of business profits, generating employment, rental of business properties, providing cheaper services, supporting formal sector businesses and payment of operating licences to municipalities.

- The major challenges to business survival and expansion include difficulties of securing start-up capital and business loans from formal financial institutions, especially banks; lack of basic business training and skills; exclusion from formal banking systems; vulnerability to xenophobic attacks and destruction of stock and businesses premises; and hostile operating environments including official harassment, extortion and demands for bribes or protection money.

- While many governments are developing plans and policies for diaspora engagement, an important information gap concerns the attitudes of diasporas themselves to engagement in development-related activities and initiatives in their countries of origin. A study of the global Zambian diaspora showed that most are interested in making private investments in Zambia, with the greatest sectoral interest in agriculture/horticulture, import/export, manufacturing, tourism and transport. Many expressed interest in contributing to development projects in Zambia related to education, healthcare, infrastructure development, childcare and microfinance initiatives.

- A study of immigrants from the SADC in Canada found that many felt they have an important role to play in developing their countries of origin. The majority remit money to their country of origin. Preferred avenues of engagement include skills transfer, investing in businesses, participation in development projects, educational exchanges, volunteer work, fundraising for development projects, philanthropy, export and import of goods to and from the country of origin, investing in infrastructural development and providing distance learning. Others specifically mentioned their desire to be involved in activities that would lead to greater empowerment for women and children.

The next section of the report examines the policy implications of the information about migration flows and development implications provided in the previous section. There was a considerable degree of unanimity among the stakeholders interviewed for this study on the importance of seeing migration as a regional development issue requiring a co-ordinated regional response in Southern Africa. There was some expectation of a difference in opinion between regional and national stakeholders. However, many of the latter were also willing to acknowledge that migration was not purely an issue of national importance. Where they differed was on who should be driving the agenda: national governments or regional bodies.

In principle, there is significant awareness among SADC member states about the need to strengthen efforts aimed at harnessing migration for inclusive growth and development. In practice, little progress has been made on mainstreaming migration and development at the national or regional policy level. Regional efforts to forge a common approach to migration appear promising but, while states appear willing to make initial commitments to agreements, instruments and initiatives, they are generally unwilling to ratify and implement anything that appears to infringe on their national sovereignty or the perceived interests of citizens.

At the regional level, there is a paucity of instruments that focus directly on migration and development. An evaluation of the SADC Secretariat's Regional Indicative Strategic Development Plan (RISDP) has concluded that "the relationship between migration and poverty is under-represented in the plan's proposed intervention areas and only addressed in a partial and circumscribed manner." Freedom of intra-regional movement has been a principle of the SADC since its foundation, although this is not explicitly tied to positive development outcomes. Despite this objective, unfettered free movement is very far from being a reality. The Secretariat has had no success in getting all member states to ratify its two major regional mobility policy initiatives: the 1995 Draft Protocol on the Free Movement of Persons and the 2005 Protocol on the Facilitation of Movement of Persons. Greater regional mobility initiatives are trumped by national immigration policies focused on movement control.

SADC member states prefer to act bilaterally in their dealings with each other on migration through instruments such as Joint Permanent Commissions (JPCs) and Memoranda of Understanding. At the level of individual member states, the mandate and expertise required for, and resources devoted to, migration management is often limited to routine and operational capacity requirements, as opposed to a more strategic approach in which migration management is an essential component of development objectives.

Little discernible progress has therefore been made with regard to the implementation of a free movement regime by the SADC Secretariat. In part, this is because there is very little data or analysis on exactly what the impact of removing border controls in the region would be. In many ways, the SADC is already a de facto free movement zone and the removal of controls would not have a massive impact on migration flows. What it would do is provide legal channels for those who want to migrate, reduce the opportunities for personal enrichment by corrupt state functionaries on both sides of borders, eliminate current high levels of corruption and abuse in the immigration system and reduce the exploitation of migrants who enjoy few rights and protections. However, free movement is likely to remain politically unpalatable to most states for the foreseeable future.

One of the key components of inclusive growth strategies is poverty reduction through productive and decent employment. Given the high levels of poverty and inequality throughout Southern Africa, it is important to view migrant employment rights as an integral part of the inclusive growth agenda. The SADC Secretariat has made various efforts to put in place instruments that commit member states to protecting the rights of migrant workers. A recent study for the United Nations Research Institute for Social Development (UNRISD) examined the issue of migrant protection and rights in the Southern African region as a whole and identified the various regional-level commitments to protecting migrant rights and the obstacles to their implementation.

This report examines various instruments including the UN Convention on the Protection of the Rights of All Migrant Workers and Members of Their Families, the Charter of Fundamental Social Rights in SADC, the SADC Code on

Social Security, ILO Conventions 87, 100, 111 and 182, the Convention Concerning Decent Work for Domestic Workers (Domestic Workers Convention), the SADC Protocol on Employment and Labour, and the SADC Regional Labour Migration Policy Framework and concludes that, as with the effort to implement freedom of movement, ratification and implementation are proving problematical as few member states are willing to ratify the appropriate instruments. A gender analysis of the various African Union (AU) and SADC strategic instruments shows that gender and migration issues feature only in piecemeal fashion.

Regional-level instruments, polices and protocols do exist, but these are barely enforced and national laws and institutions take precedence. The persistent limitations of migration governance on the continent are recognized as an obstacle to regional and continental poverty reduction. Furthermore, policies and instruments to protect migrant and gender rights are implemented within a difficult social and political context in which xenophobic and patriarchal attitudes persist. In sum, there are many challenges in advancing gender-sensitive, rights-based migration governance in the SADC region. The scale, complexity and diversity of migration, combined with incomplete and inconsistent data, make it difficult to measure and monitor the gender composition of migrant flows and stocks, or to understand the particular contributions and vulnerabilities of female migrants. A dual focus on empowerment and protection should guide programming and policy development on gender and migration in the region.

The final section of the report makes specific recommendations for a future regional programme on harnessing migration for development and inclusive growth. Given the lack of progress at regional and national level in advancing a migration and development agenda, we argue that programming should focus on "demonstration" projects that provide clear evidence of the development impacts of migration for countries of origin and destination. These projects could then be scaled up. In order to establish priority entry points, the report does three things:

- Presents the results of the stakeholder perceptions of priorities in which knowledge and information gaps were a recurrent theme;

- Analyzes and categorizes the recommendations for making migration work for development in the SDGs, the Valetta Accord and various AU and SADC agreements, protocols and instruments;

- Develops a Programming Framework (PF) consisting of 10 core migration and development issues and 27 associated potential entry points; and

This analysis leads to the identification of five major entry points in the programming framework under the general rubric of a recommended programme on Gender and Migration for Development and Inclusive Growth in Southern Africa. For each point, the report provides a detailed rationale, examples of similar programmes and likely outcomes. In summary, the five recommended entry points are as follows:

- **Entry Point One: Building a Gendered Knowledge Base on Migration.** One of the recurrent themes in the stakeholder interviews was (a) the limited public availability and utility of official data on migration; and (b) the lack of knowledge about regional migration causes, volumes, experiences and impacts. A common failing of official data and the case-study research literature is the absence of systematic and generalizable information on the gendered nature of migration. In order to provide detailed, policy-relevant, gender-disaggregated data on migration and its development impacts, a different methodological approach is needed. There is a need for the collection of national migration data at the household level in countries of origin and destination through the implementation of nationally representative surveys of migrant-sending households. The knowledge and policy value of this kind of methodology is clearly illustrated by previous projects with dated findings that are still widely cited as authoritative sources of data on all aspects of migration, including its gender dimensions. These surveys would ensure the collection of data on a range of critical migration and development issues including migration drivers, migrant characteristics and motivations, migrant occupations and remitting behaviour, remittance channels and uses, and general migration impacts at the household, community and national scales.

- **Entry Point Two: Protecting Female Migrants in Domestic Work.** The SADC Labour Migration Policy Framework has as two of its objectives (a) strengthening protection of the rights of migrant workers; and (b) harnessing positive gender considerations and demographic dividends. These objectives urgently need to be realized in the low-wage sectors in which migrant women and girls tend to concentrate, especially domestic work. A programme focus on the rights and protection of women and girl migrants would materially advance the objectives of the Framework and potentially enhance its implementation as well as that of the Domestic Workers Convention. We therefore recommend a regional programme directed at improving the conditions for women and youth migrating to and working in the domestic service sector. The extent to which employers, labour brokers and governments are in breach of the Convention is unknown and needs to be systematically researched. Further, programmes are needed to inform domestic workers of their rights and employers of their obligations. Because most migrant women in domestic work tend to move along major migration corridors there is a strong case for adopting a corridor-focused approach to programme implementation. Two corridors in particular are known to be significant avenues for migrant women in domestic work: the Zimbabwe-Gauteng-Western Cape corridor and the Lesotho-Gauteng corridor. By focusing attention on these two corridors, identifying the problems that migrant domestic workers face and that materially affect the employment conditions of migrant women, this intervention could have a strong demonstration effect on the need to protect and guarantee the rights of vulnerable workers and ensure that they benefit from inclusive economic growth.

- **Entry Point Three: Maximizing Remittance Impacts for Women Migrants.** As the primary source of income for the majority of migrant-sending households, remittance earnings are vital in enabling households to meet their basic needs. Food is the most common annual expenditure of remittance money in both male and female migrant-sending households. Remittances do not appear to be spent on non-essential or luxury items but nor are they commonly directed towards savings or investment in business or other productive activities. While there is a need for updated regional data on the gendered dimensions of remitting, the priority now is to devise practical, actionable programmes of support which would turn remittances from meeting basic household consumption needs into sources of productive investment by recipients at the household and community levels. There is considerable global and regional debate about how best to harness remittances for development and inclusive growth. The Scaling Up Remittances (SURE) programme of the International Fund for Agricultural Development (IFAD) is a potential model for this programme. However, IFAD's rural focus assumes that such programmes should concentrate on rural areas, whereas it is far more likely that the opportunities for the productive use of remittances are greater in urban areas. Thus, we suggest that programming should focus more on urban-urban remitting to have tangible results and benefits for inclusive growth.

- **Entry Point Four: Enhancing Female and Youth Migrant Entrepreneurship.** In cities throughout Southern Africa, migrants from other countries (including forced migrants) are involved in the establishment of small businesses to support themselves and their families and to generate remittances to send back to their home countries. There is a common perception that migrant entrepreneurs are "survivalists" , forced to establish their businesses because of a failure to obtain formal employment. However, there is a growing body of research that highlights the entrepreneurial orientation and motivation of the majority of migrant business owners. Studies have identified the following as major business challenges: (a) economic challenges including shortages of start-up capital, lack of access to credit, competition from formal sector outlets and suppliers' high prices; (b) social challenges such as prejudice against their nationality and xenophobic attacks; and (c) security challenges such as crime and theft, confiscation of goods by the police, harassment and demands for bribes and protection money, and physical attacks. Despite these problems, migrant entrepreneurs deliver important development benefits to countries of origin (through remittances) and destination (including cheaper foodstuffs and consumables, credit facilities, and job creation, as well as generating economic profits for formal sector suppliers such as wholesalers and supermarkets). Migrant entrepreneurs in general, and women and youth in particular, are still in need of programmes of support in order to address some of the obstacles they face and to maximize their entrepreneurial activities and contributions. There is a dearth of programmes supporting migrant youth and women's small and micro-entrepreneurship activities and initiatives in Southern Africa, particularly as migrants are generally excluded from government training and support programmes.

- **Entry Point Five: Deploying Diaspora Skills for Women/Youth Empowerment.** There is increasing interest in the actual and potential role of diasporas as a resource for development and inclusive growth in Africa. Diasporas possess five forms of diaspora capital (the "5 Cs"): intellectual capital, financial capital, political capital, cultural capital and social capital. In order for African governments and regional organizations to engage effectively with diasporas, it is important to understand what motivates diasporas to be involved in African development: the "3 Ps" of pecuniary interests, private interests and public philanthropic interests. The global Southern African diaspora represents a large skills and expertise pool, several million strong, that has not yet been effectively leveraged for development by

Southern African countries. A regional diaspora engagement policy for Southern Africa as a whole needs to be based on (a) a mapping of existing development-related initiatives by members of diasporas from Southern Africa; (b) information about the types of engagement activities that members of the diaspora are interested in supporting or participating in at the regional level; and (c) the establishment of mechanisms which would enable and facilitate engagement at the regional level, perhaps initially in the form of a platform or marketplace for supporting regional projects. To align this proposal with the general theme of gender and migration, such a programme could focus on diaspora support for projects that aim to enhance gender equity and the empowerment of women and girls.

CHAPTER 1:
GOAL AND OBJECTIVES

The primary goal of this study is to present the results of a comprehensive scope of key opportunities and challenges for harnessing migration for inclusive growth and development at the regional level in Southern Africa.[1] The main objectives of the study were as follows:

- Provide an overview of regional migration stocks and flows identifying regional trends, drivers and impacts from existing research literature and official data;

- Profile migrant characteristics at the regional level including demographic composition, types of migration and occupational profile;

- Examine the relevance of multilateral, continental and regional migration instruments, policies, protocols, agreements and forums with a view to identifying actions required to move the regional migration management agenda forward and align with the goal of enhancing migration for inclusive growth and development in Southern Africa;

- Analyze the key initiatives, opportunities and obstacles to developing a coherent, integrated and rights-regarding approach to migration management including areas of common commitment and ownership, and points of actual and potential conflict and disagreement between states;

- Conduct a gender analysis of regional migration dynamics including gender dimensions of migration, challenges, dangers and vulnerabilities confronting migrant women and other vulnerable groups and gender analysis of migration management in Southern Africa; and

- Inventory current regional migration initiatives by governments, inter-governmental agencies, the private sector, civil society and other development partners and identify potential programming areas that are weak or underdeveloped.

CHAPTER 2: METHODOLOGY

The report relies on data and information from four main sources:

- Existing research literature and data on regional migration dynamics and trends in Southern Africa. The research literature is voluminous but generally adopts a small-area, small-sample case study approach which raises questions of representativeness.

- Official data, where current and available, to identify current patterns, trends and types of migration. The International Organization for Migration (IOM) recently reviewed these official sources in Southern Africa and concludes that there are "huge gaps" in the data available for the construction of a regional migration picture.[2] There is currently no facility in Southern Africa for the central collection and analysis of migration data at the regional level.

- Bilateral global migration data sets compiled by international organizations and agencies. Those used in this report include:

    - United Nations Population Division Bilateral International Migration Stock 1990-2015

    - World Bank Migration and Remittances: Bilateral Remittance Matrix 2015

    - World Bank Remittance Prices Worldwide Database

- Field research involving key informant interviews and consultations with stakeholders including international organizations and donors, national government departments, and representatives from civil society, business, labour and the academy.[3] The fieldwork was undertaken by a team of four fieldworkers from Southern Hemisphere Consulting. Four country visits were undertaken to South Africa, Mozambique, Botswana and Zimbabwe. Regional interviews were conducted face to face, telephonically and by email. A total of 60 interviews were conducted with 86 interviewees. All interviews were transcribed and analyzed using NVIVO software.

CHAPTER 3: CONTEXTUAL ANALYSIS: REGIONAL MIGRATION IN SOUTHERN AFRICA

INTRODUCTION

There are a number of reasons why migration should be considered a *regional* issue, challenge and opportunity in Southern Africa requiring a regionally co-ordinated response:

- Cross-border movements of people constitute one of the major mechanisms of regional integration in Southern Africa (along with trade and investment). Goods and capital move relatively freely and legally across the region but people still face considerable barriers to movement;

- Vast differences in levels of development and employment opportunities across the region have led to extremely uneven migration flows.[4] All countries both send and receive migrants but the balance between the two varies significantly. Zimbabwe was a major destination before 2000 but has since become the region's single largest exporter of migrants.[5]

- Temporary, circular migration is the norm in the region with migrants retaining close ties with home countries and communities through formal and informal transfers of cash and goods in the form of remittances. In effect, migration and remittances have become a major source of development finance across the region.

- The majority of migration movements within and to the Southern African region fall into the category of South-South migration. This form of migration, from one developing country to another, can have positive and simultaneous development and inclusive growth impacts on both countries of origin and destination.

- From a migration management perspective, regional organizations have recognized the importance of regional harmonization and co-ordinated action. However, governments have been slower to recognize the reality of regional migration, leading to a disjuncture between initiatives to facilitate movement and co-ordinate at the continental and regional level, and national governments that wish to avoid any binding commitment to regional migration processes and instruments.

MIGRATION WITHIN SOUTHERN AFRICA

Migration Patterns

There is a common perception that Southern Africa is experiencing a major increase in migration numbers. However, UN migrant stock data for the region calls this into question. The total number of migrants in the SADC has remained relatively stable since 1990 at around 4.5 million people (Table 1). There have certainly been shifts within the region, with

TABLE 1: TOTAL MIGRANT STOCK OF SOUTHERN AFRICAN COUNTRIES, 1990-2015

	1990	1995	2000	2005	2010	2015	% Change 1990-2015
Angola	33,517	39,813	46,108	61,329	76,549	106,845	+218%
Botswana	27,510	40,168	57,064	88,829	120,912	160,644	+484%
DRC	129,527	191,635	305,002	315,238	419,649	392,996	+203%
Lesotho	8,240	7,240	6,167	6,290	6,414	6,572	-20%
Madagascar	23,917	21,177	23,451	26,058	28,905	32,075	+34%
Mauritius	3,613	7,493	15,543	19,647	24,836	28,585	+691%
Malawi	1,127,724	241,624	232,620	221,661	217,722	215,158	-618%
Mozambique	122,332	168,256	195,702	204,830	214,612	222,928	-81%
Namibia	120,641	115,372	134,403	106,274	102,405	93,888	+82%
Seychelles	3,721	5,148	6,574	8,997	11,420	12,791	+244%
South Africa	1,163,883	1,003,807	1,001,825	1,210,936	1,943,009	2,309,044[6]	+98%
Swaziland	72,085	25,031	22,855	27,097	30,476	31,579	-56%
Tanzania	574,025	1,106,043	928,180	770,846	308,600	261,222	-54%
Zambia	279,029	244,338	321,167	252,749	149,637	127,915	-54%
Zimbabwe	626,821	431,226	410,041	392,693	397,891	398,866	-36%
Total	4,316,585	3,648,471	3,706,702	3,713,474	4,053,037	4,401,018	+2%

Source: United Nations Population Division (2015). Data retrieved on June 10, 2016 from http://www.un.org/en/development/desa/population/migration/data/

seven countries now hosting fewer migrants than they did in 1990 and seven hosting more. The greatest proportional increases in migrant stock have been in Botswana, Angola, Mauritius, the Seychelles, the DRC and South Africa. The greatest absolute increase has been in South Africa from 1.1 million to 2.3 million people. South Africa has become the major migration destination, from 29% of all migrants in the region in 1990 to 52% in 2015.

A second common perception is that the countries of Southern Africa are either migrant origin or migrant destination countries. In fact, all of the states of Southern Africa both send and receive migrants (Table 2). However, only three countries (Botswana, South Africa and Tanzania) receive more migrants than they send. With the exception of the three island states, every country has at least some migrants from every other country in the region. In addition, migrants from one country do not go to only one other country: Mozambicans and South Africans are the most dispersed (living in 10 other countries), followed by Congolese and Zambians (nine other countries), Malawians and Zimbabweans (eight other countries), and the rest in six or seven other countries. Notably, given the common perception that South Africa is only a destination country, there are 107,000 South Africans in other countries in the region. In practice, this means that all countries should have a vested interest in addressing both inward and outward migration.

Contract Mine Migration

Historically, the major form of labour migration in Southern Africa has been legal contract migration to the South African and Zimbabwean gold and coal mines, the Zambian and DRC copper mines, and the Swaziland asbestos mine. The South African gold and platinum mines continue to employ migrants from other countries, particularly Lesotho, Mozambique and Swaziland. However, mine closures and retrenchments, employment levels in the mining industry have been falling for two decades. Between 1987 and 2010, the number of mineworkers fell from 477,000 to 215,000. No new migrant mineworkers have been hired from outside South Africa since 2003. The proportion of the mine workforce from outside South Africa fell from 60% in 2003 to only 23% in 2013. The Employment Bureau of Africa (TEBA) estimates that by 2023 there will be no foreign migrants on the South African mines, thus bringing to an end the contract labour system that began in the 1890s.[7] One of the major consequences of the phasing out of contract migration has been an increase in unregulated migration. With households and communities no longer able to depend on mine jobs and mine remittances, people migrate informally to work in other sectors, including commercial agriculture, domestic work, construction, the informal sector and illicit mining.

The decline of migrant mineworkers from neighbouring countries has led to:

- A decline in remittance flows to these areas from the mines;

- New forms of migration among former mineworkers including their participation in dangerous but lucrative illicit mining in abandoned mines; and

- Internal and informal cross-border migration by young workseekers, including increasing numbers of women, from these areas in search of non-mine employment.

TABLE 2: SADC MIGRANTS IN OTHER SADC COUNTRIES, 2015

	As Origin	As Destination	Net Migration
Mozambique	616,945	135,586	-481,359
Zimbabwe	602,844	249,789	-353,055
Lesotho	362,000	3,040	-358,960
Malawi	280,077	153,189	-126,888
Angola	271,838	51,981	-219,857
DRC	195,946	185,205	-10,741
Zambia	164,033	75,683	-88,350
Namibia	138,353	63,206	-75,147
South Africa	107,029	1,803,163	+1,696,134
Swaziland	92,232	23,450	-68,782
Botswana	51,832	105,998	+54,166
Tanzania	35,891	92,782	+56,891
Madagascar	4,182	n/a	n/a
Mauritius	11,856	3,023	+8,833
Seychelles	1,530	1,614	-84
Source: United Nations Population Division (2015). Data retrieved on June 10, 2016 from http://www.un.org/en/development/desa/population/migration/data/			

The economic challenges include rising unemployment and the creation of alternative job opportunities for young workseekers. There is little evidence that the supplier governments have seriously addressed these challenges. In Lesotho, this may be because the growth of the textile industry has ameliorated the overall impact by providing employment to over 50,000 women.

Refugee Migration

The number of forced migrants within Southern Africa peaked at 1.8 million in 1992. The numbers have declined in the last 20 years to their present level of 142,000 (mostly from the DRC) (Figure 1). Less than 10% of the region's total migrant stock therefore comprises refugees from within the region. The number of refugees from crisis states in Africa outside the region has also declined, peaking in the late 1990s at around 700,000 and declining to less than 100,000 in 2012 (Figure 2). Most countries have seen a decline in their refugee population although South Africa's has slowly increased over the last decade to its current level (2015) of 110,000 (mainly from African countries such as Somalia, Ethiopia and the Great Lakes region).

Governments are known to cite asylum-seeker figures to build a case that they are being inundated by refugees. The South African government has often claimed that it has over 1 million asylum-seekers in the country.[8] A corrective to this misinformation in South Africa's new Green Paper clarifies that this actually refers to the cumulative number of asylum applications received over time and that the number of currently active applications for asylum is only 78,000.[9] The number of new asylum-seekers did increase dramatically after 2000, peaking in South Africa at 222,000 in 2009 (Table 3). Since 2012, the number of asylum-seekers has been around 60,000-70,000 per annum. The main countries of origin in 2015 were Zimbabwe (10,854), Ethiopia (9,322), Nigeria (6,554), DRC (6,355), Bangladesh (3,290), Pakistan (2,448), Malawi (2,372), India (1,728), Somalia (1,582) and Ghana (1,778).[10]

For the past decade, asylum-seeking has been dominated by migrants from Zimbabwe, with as many as 80% of asylum-seekers in 2011, and 44% overall between 2002 and 2015. There is disagreement over how many asylum-seekers are refugees and how many are economic migrants. The South African government has claimed that 90% are economic migrants, while some researchers put the figure at only 50%.[11]

On the basis of the 90% claim, South Africa's new Green Paper proposes a controversial overhaul of the refugee protection system which would make it far more difficult for migrants to claim asylum, remove their right to pursue an economic livelihood, and confine asylum-seekers to "reception centres" until their cases are adjudicated.

FIGURE 1: TOTAL NUMBER OF REFUGEES IN SOUTHERN AFRICA FROM OTHER SOUTHERN AFRICAN COUNTRIES, 1970-2014

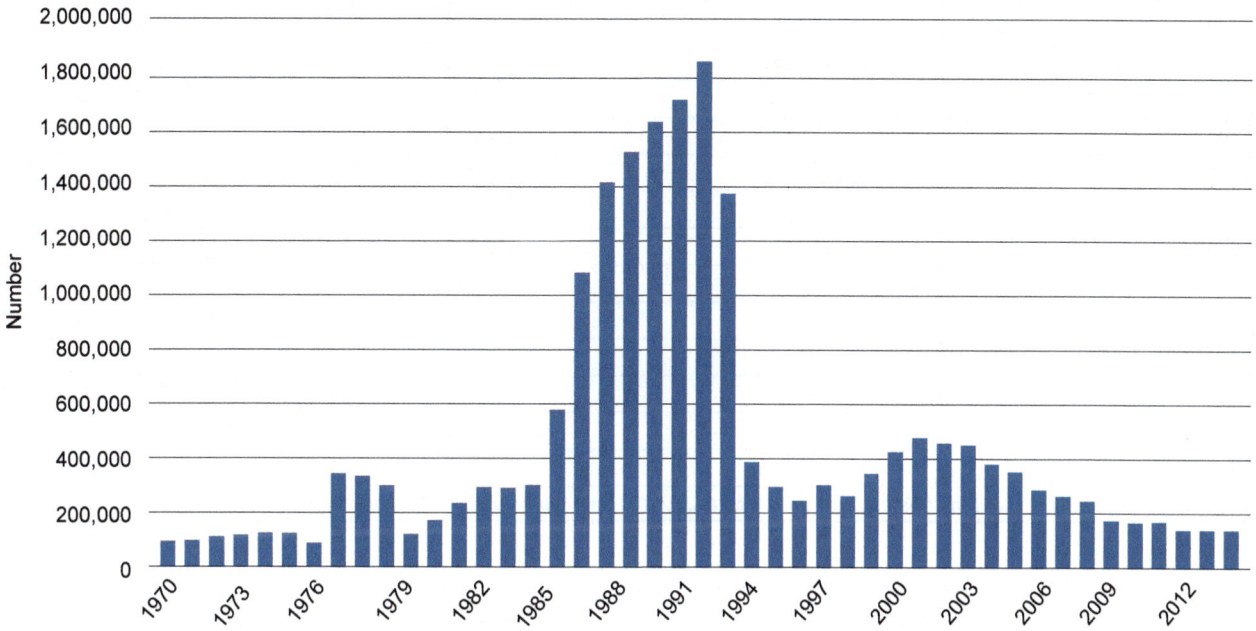

Source: UNHCR Population Statistics. Data retrieved on 12 June 2016 from http://popstats.unhcr.org/en/time_series

FIGURE 2: TOTAL NUMBER OF REFUGEES IN SOUTHERN AFRICA FROM OUTSIDE SOUTHERN AFRICA, 1985-2014

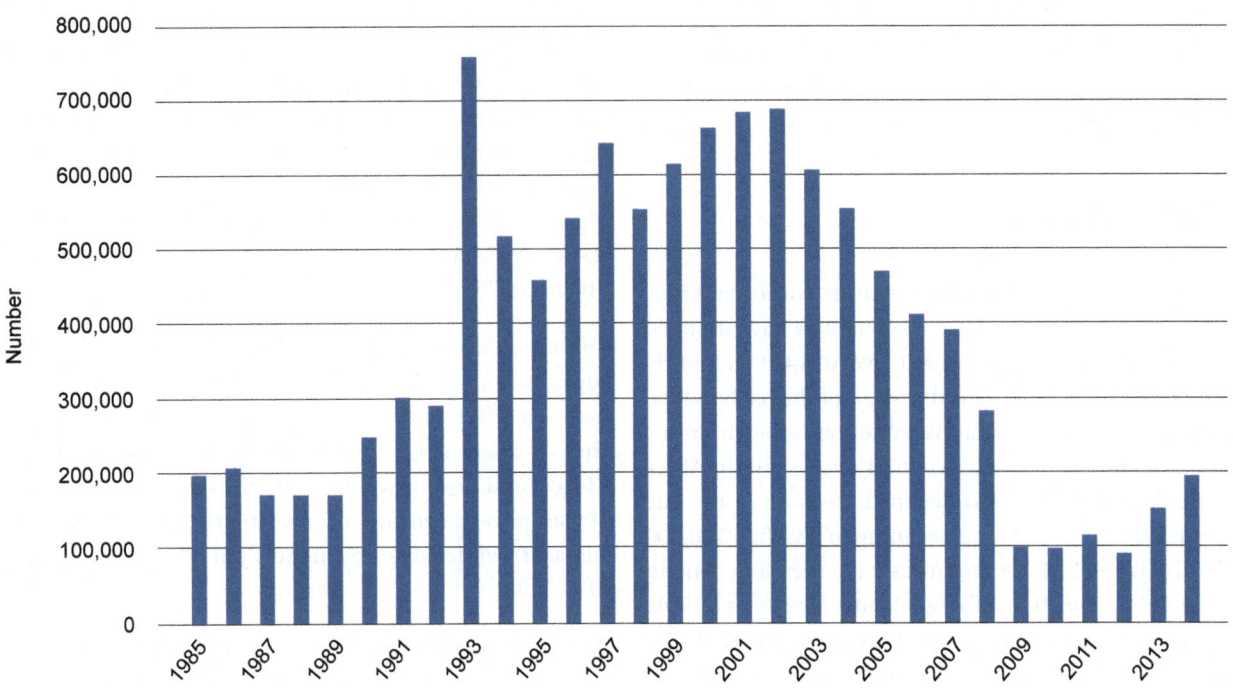

Source: UNHCR Population Statistics. Data retrieved on 12 June 2016 from http://popstats.unhcr.org/en/time_series

TABLE 3: ASYLUM APPLICATIONS IN SOUTH AFRICA, 2002-2015

Year	Total	Zimbabweans	% Zimbabwean
2002	55,426	115	0.2
2003	35,920	2,588	7.2
2004	32,565	5,789	17.8
2005	28,522	7,783	27.3
2006	53,361	18,973	35.6
2007	45,637	17,667	38.7
2008	207,206	111,968	54.0
2009	222,324	149,453	67.2
2010	180,637	146,566	81.1
2011	106,904	51,031	47.7
2012	117,187	20,842	17.8
2013	79,325	16,670	21.0
2014	84,174	20,405	24.2
2015	76,110	17,785	23.4
Total	1,325,298	587,635	44.3

Source: Source: UNHCR Population Statistics. Data retrieved on 15 July 2016 from http://popstats.unhcr.org/en/time_series

Increased Intra-Regional Mobility

Greater regional integration has led to a dramatic increase in short-term cross-border movement within Southern Africa in the past two decades and this is likely to continue. Most border-crossers are issued with visitor, tourist or business permits at the point of entry. Some countries issue short-term multiple-entry "border passes" and some permits allow multiple entry. The most important reasons for temporary movement include: (a) cross-border shopping; (b) informal cross-border informal trade (ICBT) where goods are purchased in one country for sale in the home country; (c) formal business; (d) tourism; (e) visiting friends and relatives; and (e) medical migration. While short-term border crossing for these purposes is not generally classified as a form of migration, this conclusion needs to be qualified in Southern Africa. First, transactional data on border-crossing includes many migrants who use visitor and other permits to enter legally into another country. Second, certain categories, such as informal traders, can be viewed as circular migrants because they move with great frequency and may cumulatively be away from their home country for an extended period during the year.

Mixed Migration

The term mixed migration is increasingly used by the IOM, United Nations High Commissioner for Refugees (UNHCR) and governments to suggest that forced (refugee) migrants and economic ("illegal" or "irregular") migrants use the same migration corridors and are indistinguishable from one another. To define mixed migration in this dualistic way fails to capture the complexity of migrant movements in Southern Africa. A more appropriate and inclusive definition should move beyond the legal status of migrants, as defined by states, to consider all aspects of the migration process.[12] Migration streams from one country to another within Southern Africa are increasingly heterogeneous, encompassing diverse motives and reasons for migration, different forms of cross-border movement, various legal and extra-legal categories and diverse migrant characteristics. However, the major change in migration patterns in the past 20 years has been a significant increase in cross-border movement for livelihood reasons.

This is particularly evident in the case of migration from Zimbabwe, which has seen an upsurge in migrants of all ages and skills levels.[13] Although some migration is long-term or permanent, most is not with the intention of settling in the destination country. As in the past, much migration is circular in character with migrants retaining strong economic and emotional ties with the home country.[14]

Data from the South African Census 2011 is illustrative of the growing heterogeneity of migrant streams:[15]

- Other SADC countries are the dominant source of migrants to South Africa (68%) but there are increasing numbers of South-South migrants from the rest of Africa (7%) and from Asia (5%);

- The migrant population pyramid shows that only half of all migrants are of prime working-age (25-44) while 12% are over the age of 55 and 18% are youth aged 15-24. The migration of unaccompanied minors and increased family migration accounts for the 9% of migrant children under the age of 14;

- Income levels vary significantly with roughly half of all migrants in the lowest two income quintiles, 34% in the middle-income quintile and 14% in the upper quintiles; and

- The educational levels of migrants varies considerably. Over 60% of migrants from other SADC countries have only some secondary school education or less (Figure 3). Around 30% have completed secondary school with 10% having post-secondary qualifications. Over 50% of migrants from the rest of Africa have completed secondary school with 25% holding a post-secondary qualification.

Informal Migration

Informal migration (sometimes called irregular or undocumented migration) occurs primarily because most Southern African countries do not provide work permits to semi-skilled and low-skilled migrants from other countries. This has the potential to change if the proposals in the new South African Green Paper are implemented. Migration in Southern Africa has become increasingly informal and unregulated, with a growing proportion of economic migrants moving across borders and adopting a wide variety of practices to legalize their movement or to manipulate existing systems of control and enforcement. These include:

- Entering another country legally on visitor's permits and then finding work, either letting the permit expire or returning home regularly to renew the permit;

- Entering into informal agreements with employers and labour brokers to bring them into a country to work for a set period and then return home;

FIGURE 3: EDUCATION LEVELS OF MIGRANTS IN SOUTH AFRICA

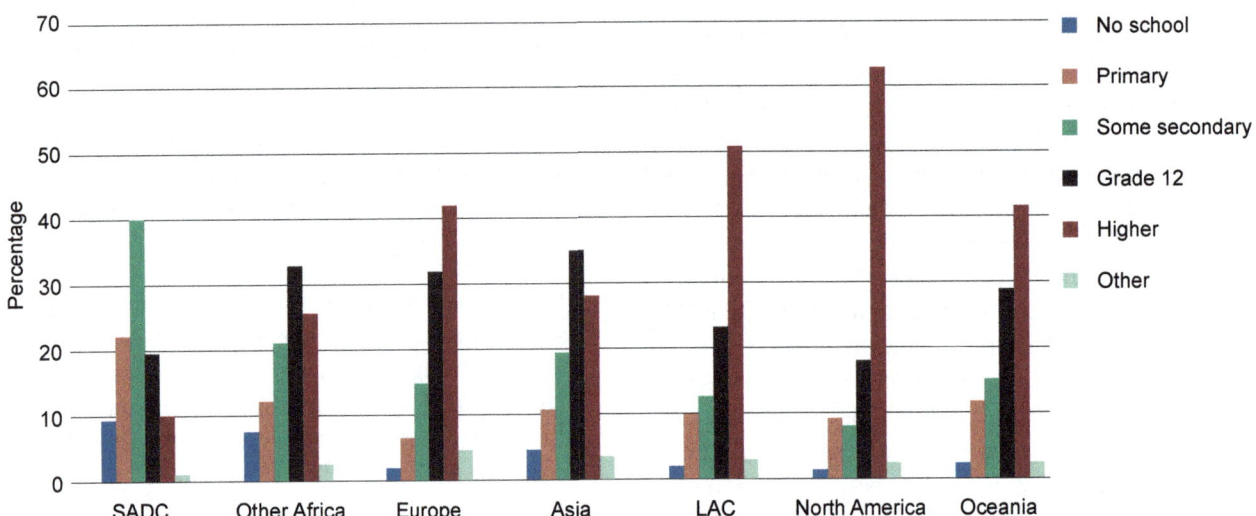

Source: SSA, Census 2011

- Obtaining an asylum-seeker permit on arrival which legalizes stay in another country and can, in cases including South Africa, entitle the holder to work;

- Clandestine border-crossing without proper documentation, a strategy that is used mostly by those who cannot afford passports but can involve significant costs in paying guides and bribes to officials; and

- Obtaining false documentation from individuals, often state officials, willing to supply it.

The number of migrants in each of these categories is unknown. One of the challenges of measurement and management is that most are temporary migrants who return home relatively frequently. The strength of the linkages that migrants maintain with the home household, community and country therefore directly affects whether, and to what extent, the benefits of migration flow across borders. The best evidence for strong linkages comes from household surveys done by the Southern African Migration Programme (SAMP) in five Southern African countries, which found extremely regular patterns of home visits and strong links with countries of origin.[16] Of the 4,647 migrants surveyed, for example, nearly 90% returned home at least once a year, with 67% returning several times a year, and 30% returning once a month. Only 7% of migrants were away from home for longer than a year at a time.

There is no co-ordinated policy response to informalized migration at the regional level. At the national level there are various policy responses:

- Laissez faire approach, which implicitly recognizes the advantages to employers of hiring migrants without official work permits and/or lacks the capacity to manage this form of migration;

- Punitive approach involving arrest and deportation, which has been the dominant policy response in Botswana and South Africa. South Africa has deported 2.3 million migrants since 2000, over 98% to other countries in the Southern African region, at considerable cost to the state, with disruption and abuse of migrants, and with little discernible effect on migration flows;[17]

- Managerial approach, which seeks to manage migration through the issue of permits to employers, such as corporate permits issued to farmers in South Africa; and

- Regularization approach, which legalizes the status of migrants by offering them permanent residence or temporary residence and work permits. In South Africa, there have been immigration amnesties for 50,000 migrant gold miners (1995); 125,000 SADC migrants (1996); 100,000 Mozambican ex-refugees (2000) and 275,000 Zimbabweans (2010). Another amnesty for Lesotho migrants in South Africa is currently in progress. As many as 400,000 applications were expected but only 2,500 had been received by the closing date.[18]

In South Africa, regularization of the legal status of over 500,000 migrants since the mid-1990s has meant greater security and improved protection from exploitation and deportation. However, the evidence suggests that regularized status is used strategically by migrants who still maintain strong ties with home. Most other countries in the region tend to adopt either a punitive or laissez faire approach to unregulated migration.

Occupational Profile

Regional data on the occupational profile of migrants is not available for the whole region. Some countries, such as Botswana, South Africa and Zambia, published their data on the occupations of migrants at the time of the most recent census.

The 2011 South African Census found that 63% of employed migrants were in the formal sector and two-thirds were from other Southern African countries, with 10% from Europe, 7% from other African countries and 6% from Asia.[19] Unusually in international terms, migrants to South Africa appear to have a lower unemployment rate than people born in the country. Census 2011 recorded that 63% of migrants in South Africa were employed, 17% were unemployed and 20% were not economically active.[20] Data from the Quarterly

Labour Force Survey (QLFS) for 2012 shows that 15% of migrants were unemployed, compared to 26% of non-migrants and 33% of internal migrants.[21] Migrants' higher employment levels are accounted for in part by informal work and self-employment, but some South African employers also prefer hiring migrants if they are available, claiming they are cheaper or work harder.

An analysis of 2008 National Income Dynamics Study (NIDS) data compared the employment sectors of South Africans and migrants and found that with the exception of mining (with a greater relative proportion of migrants) and services (vice-versa) there were considerable similarities (Table 4).[22] The analysis showed that migrants are also distributed across the labour market and not confined to one or two sectors. Finally, a comparison with QLFS 2012 data suggests a major decline in mining employment (as anticipated) and increase in wholesale and retail, construction and agricultural employment among migrants.[23]

A similar pattern of broad distribution of migrant occupations emerges in the occupational profile of the employed

TABLE 4: EMPLOYMENT SECTORS OF MIGRANTS AND SOUTH AFRICAN CITIZENS

	NIDS (2008)		QLFS (2012)
	Local (%)	Migrant (%)	Migrant (%)
Mining and quarrying	4	15	4
Wholesale and retail	13	14	28
Manufacturing	15	13	11
Services	23	13	13
Financial	11	11	9
Private households	9	10	12
Construction	5	6	12
Agriculture	7	4	8
Transport	4	2	3
Utilities	1	1	0
Source: Budlender (2013); Fauvelle-Aymar (2014)			

TABLE 5: OCCUPATIONS OF MIGRANTS AND SOUTH AFRICANS

	NIDS (2008)		QLFS 2012
	Local (%)	Migrant (%)	Migrant (%)
Craft and related trade workers	14	33	22
Professionals	13	17	6
Low-skilled elementary	21	15	22
Clerks	11	10	4
Service and sales workers	13	9	16
Plant and machinery operators	10	8	5
Technicians and associated	5	4	7
Skilled agricultural	5	2	1
Legislators/managers/senior officials	6	1	11
Domestic workers			7
Source: Budlender (2013); Fauvelle-Aymar (2014)			

migrant population with, again, several shifts between 2008 and 2012 with a greater proportion of migrants in less-skilled jobs (Table 5).

Published data from the Zambian 2011 Census lists the top 10 occupations of migrants and shows that at least a third were in skilled job categories (Figure 4).[24] Another quarter were involved in agricultural production as farmers and workers. A more recent study has shown that Zambia is a popular destination for Chinese workers employed by Chinese companies on major infrastructural projects.[25]

Migration Corridors

Unlike the migration corridors that connect the countries of South East Asia to the Gulf, most migrants in Southern Africa travel overland and generally do so independently. The transaction costs associated with migration therefore tend to be much lower in this region and the high degrees of migration-related indebtedness in Asia are not seen in Southern Africa. However, migration is not a cost-neutral exercise and involves transportation costs, documentation fees (passports and visas), the costs of border-crossing (legal and clandestine) and the various financial demands of remaining a migrant (including fees for permit renewal, bribes and protection money).

Because of the prevalence of overland travel, migration routes tend to follow major transportation arteries. Migrants who live far from these arteries first make their way to the nearest centre on the artery where they join the flows of people leaving and returning. Destinations tend to be determined by where work or other economic opportunities are seen as most promising. Small towns and farms along a migration corridor are common temporary stopping points. Migrants moving to South Africa tend to go mainly to Gauteng, KwaZulu-Natal and the Western Cape. Social networks are exercising an increasingly strong influence on migrant destinations.

Major migration corridors include:

- Zimbabwe (Harare) through Beitbridge to farms in Limpopo, to Gauteng (Johannesburg) and to the Western Cape (Cape Town);

- Southern Zimbabwe (Bulawayo) through Plumtree to Botswana (Francistown and Gaborone). Some onward migration occurs from Botswana to South Africa;

- Southern Mozambique (rural and Maputo) through Ressano Garcia to farms in Mpumalanga, to Gauteng (Johannesburg and Pretoria) and the gold and platinum mines; and

FIGURE 4: TOP TEN MIGRANT OCCUPATIONS IN ZAMBIA

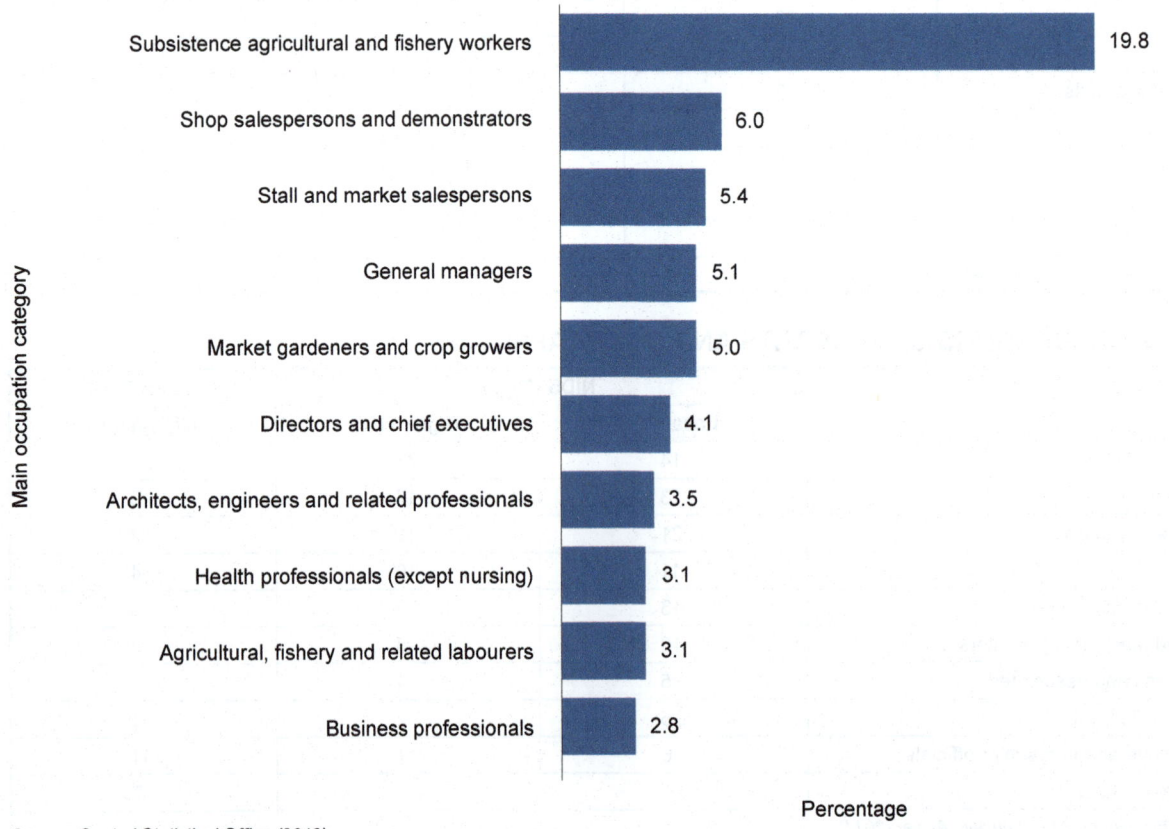

Source: Central Statistical Office (2013)

- Lesotho (rural and Maseru) through Maseru Bridge to farms and mines in the Free State, farms in the Western Cape and KwaZulu-Natal and to Bloemfontein and Gauteng (Johannesburg) for domestic workers.

MIGRATION TO SOUTHERN AFRICA

For much of the 20th century, Southern Africa was a significant destination for immigrants from Europe. After independence, most countries abandoned these colonial policies. Permanent immigration from Europe was also largely abandoned by South Africa after 1994 and it joined the other countries of the region in rejecting immigration policies as a way to attract skilled migrants. In 2014, for example, South Africa issued only 4,136 permanent residence permits of which only 30% (1,228) were work-related.[26] Economic migration from the rest of Africa, as well as Asia, has increased significantly in the last two decades. A quarter of all migrants in Southern Africa are now from African countries outside the region (Table 6). A further 2% are from Asia but the numbers are increasing rapidly. The majority of the 7% of migrants from Europe are a legacy from an earlier era when the government recruited immigrants from Europe to add to the white population.

The fact that one-third of migrants in the Southern African region are not from the region raises two pertinent questions: (a) is the historical legacy of colonialism and apartheid acting as a disincentive for SADC countries to fully engage with and compete on an increasingly global market for skills? and (b) should the SADC be trying to build a regional policy that gives preference to intra-regional migrants and excludes migrants from other African regions or should it rather be co-operating with other regions to pursue and implement an Africa-wide agenda under AU direction?

Most countries in Southern Africa issue temporary work permits to skilled migrants from inside and outside the region, provided that employers can demonstrate that no local can do the job. None operate a points system and most are unlikely to issue permanent immigration status. There is actually a major disjuncture between independent assessments of skills shortages and the heavily bureaucratic mechanisms in place in most countries to control the import of skills. This is particularly evident in the health sector where skills import is not seen as a viable solution to the shortage of health professionals.

Comprehensive regional data on skills migration is currently unavailable. Data that does exist suggests that most skilled migrants in Southern Africa come from outside the region. South Africa, for example, issued 96,000 work permits between 2011 and 2014. In 2014, around a quarter went to Zimbabweans but no other Southern African states are in the top 10 origin countries (Figure 5).[27] The majority of Botswana's 20,000 work permit holders are from neighbouring Zimbabwe and South Africa (Figure 6). In the case of Zambia, the picture is somewhat different with the majority of work permits issued to migrants from China and India.[28]

MIGRATION FROM SOUTHERN AFRICA

There is a common perception that migration in Southern Africa largely occurs within and to the region. It is therefore important to emphasize that there has been significant out-migration from Southern Africa. Although comprehensive data for every country is not available, there is abundant evidence that the region has experienced a major "brain drain" of skills in the past two decades and that this is ongoing. Recent surveys, particularly in the health sector, show extreme levels of dissatisfaction and a high emigration potential among health professionals.[29] If these push factors

TABLE 6: REGION OF ORIGIN OF MIGRANTS IN SOUTHERN AFRICA, 2015

	No.	%
Southern Africa	2,840,331	65.6
East, West and Central Africa	1,090,733	25.2
Europe	284,919	6.6
Asia	68,158	1.6
North Africa and Middle East	18,376	0.4
North America	15,982	0.3
Oceania	5,298	0.1
South America	3,950	0.1
Source: United Nations Population Division (2015). Data retrieved on June 10, 2016 from http://www.un.org/en/development/desa/population/migration/data/		

FIGURE 5: COUNTRY OF ORIGIN OF NEW WORK PERMIT HOLDERS IN SOUTH AFRICA, 2014

N=24 027

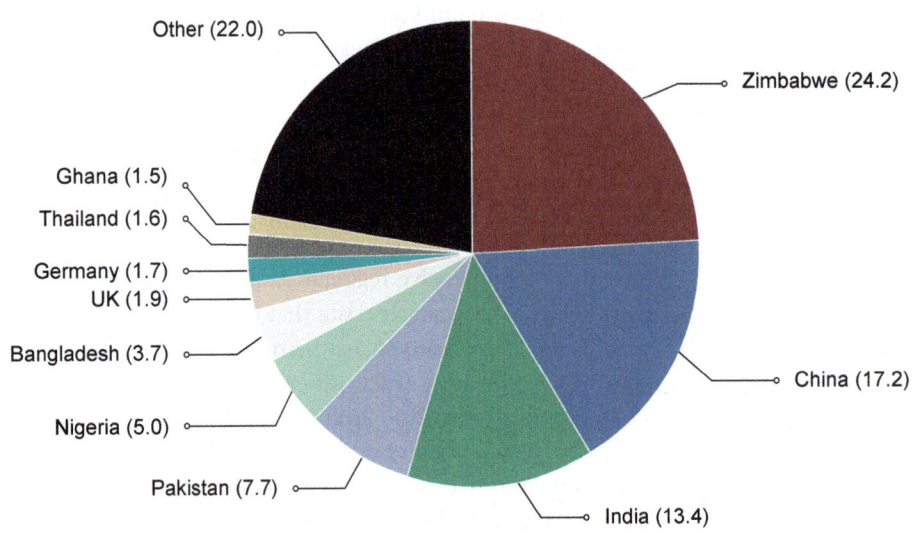

Source: Documented Immigrants in South Africa 2014 (Pretoria: Statistics South Africa, 2015).

FIGURE 6: COUNTRY OF ORIGIN OF WORK PERMIT HOLDERS IN BOTSWANA, 2012

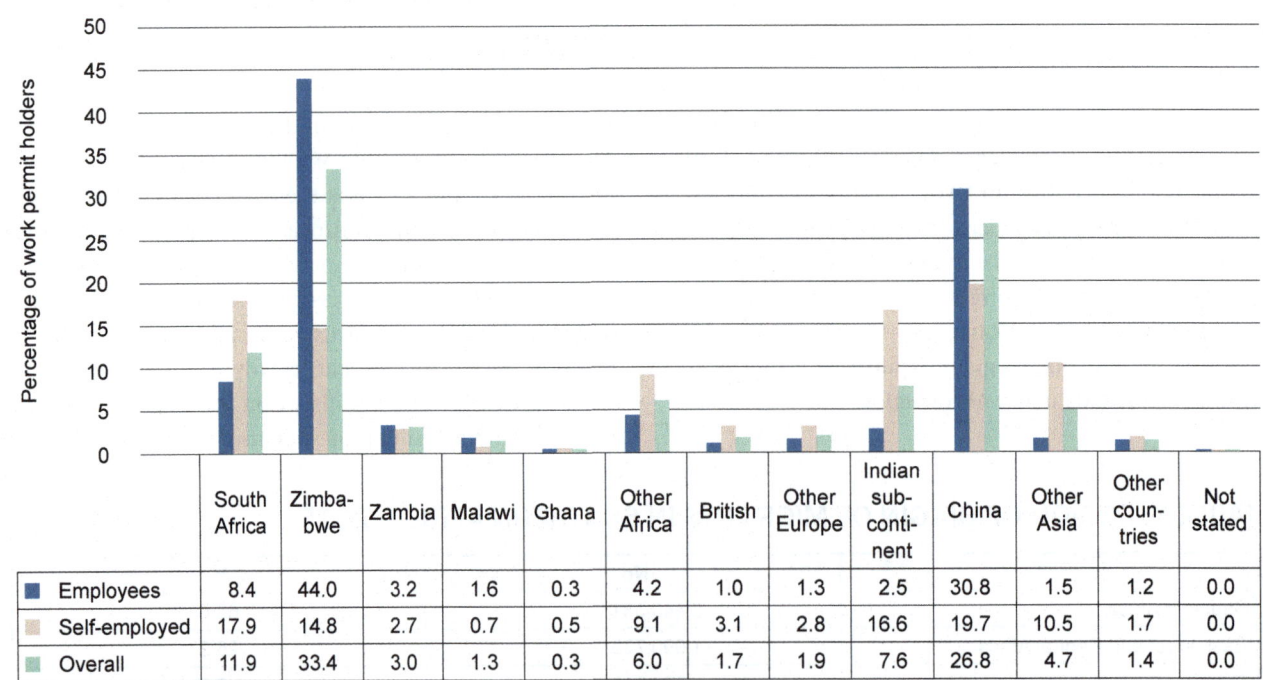

	South Africa	Zimba-bwe	Zambia	Malawi	Ghana	Other Africa	British	Other Europe	Indian sub-conti-nent	China	Other Asia	Other coun-tries	Not stated
■ Employees	8.4	44.0	3.2	1.6	0.3	4.2	1.0	1.3	2.5	30.8	1.5	1.2	0.0
Self-employed	17.9	14.8	2.7	0.7	0.5	9.1	3.1	2.8	16.6	19.7	10.5	1.7	0.0
Overall	11.9	33.4	3.0	1.3	0.3	6.0	1.7	1.9	7.6	26.8	4.7	1.4	0.0

Country of origin

Source: Statistics Botswana, Work Permits Holders, Third Quarter 2012 (Gaborone, 2014)

FIGURE 7: COUNTRY OF ORIGIN OF WORK PERMIT HOLDERS IN ZAMBIA, 2009-2012

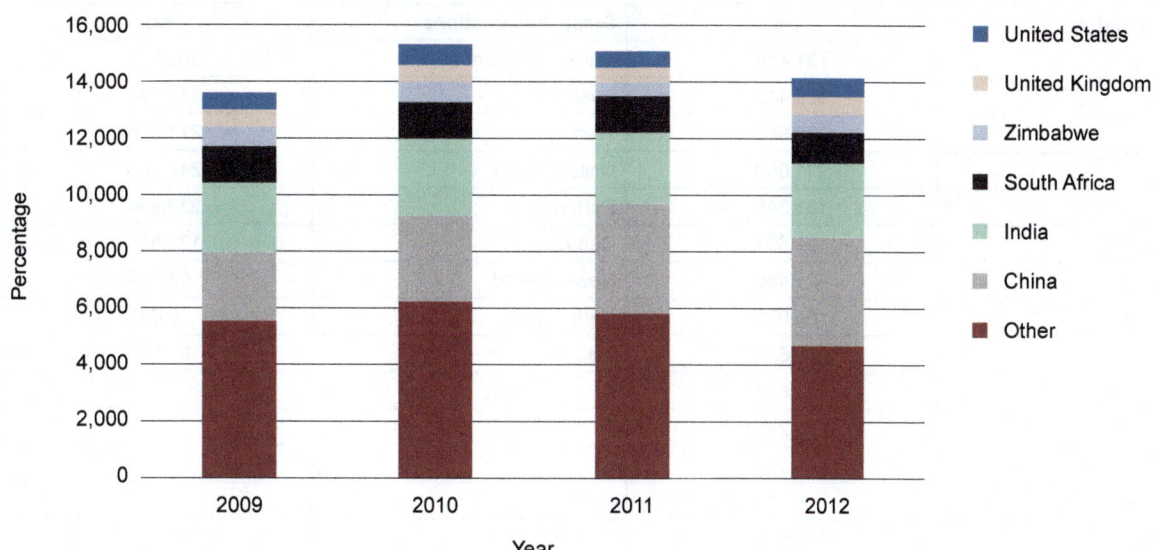

are not addressed by governments, the drain of skills from the region is very likely to continue.

The movement of migrants out of the region is so voluminous that 53% (or 6.0 million people) of the total number of Southern African migrants are outside the region (Table 7). This means that there are *more* Southern African migrants outside than inside the region, with 1.2 million (21%) in Europe, 1.1 million (19%) in East and Central Africa, 374,000 (6%) in North America and 309,000 (5%) in Oceania. This has considerable implications for migration and development policies which align with global and African advocacy of the role of diasporas in African development.

With the exception of the BLS states (Botswana, Lesotho and Swaziland) and Namibia, all of the SADC countries have sizable diasporas outside the continent. The South African diaspora is the largest (at 730,000), followed by Zimbabwe

(380,000), Angola (238,000), the DRC (211,000), Mauritius (151,000), Madagascar (134,000), Tanzania (121,000), Mozambique (85,000) and Zambia (74,000). This suggests that most Southern African countries have an interest in diaspora engagement for development. In terms of the geographical spread of the SADC diaspora, the greatest concentration is in the UK, followed by Australia, France, the US, Portugal, Canada, New Zealand, the Netherlands and Germany.

The major diaspora migration corridors are South Africa to the UK and Australia, followed by Angola to Portugal, Zimbabwe to the UK, Madagascar to France and South Africa to the US. In total, there are 10 bilateral diaspora corridors with more than 45,000 migrants from Southern Africa, again suggesting that a broader regional diaspora migration policy or set of policies would be a productive way forward.

TABLE 7: DESTINATION OF SOUTHERN AFRICAN MIGRANTS, 2015

	No.	%
Southern Africa	2,840,331	47.0
Europe	1,240,557	20.5
Rest of Africa	1,172,778	19.4
North America	374,295	6.2
Oceania	308,706	5.1
South America	69,201	1.1
North Africa and Middle East	15,600	0.3
Asia	10,573	0.2
West Africa	8,992	0.1
	6,041,033	100.0

TABLE 8: DIASPORA ORIGINS AND LOCATIONS, 2015

Diaspora Origins	No.	Diaspora Locations	No.
South Africa	731,416	United Kingdom	540,915
Zimbabwe	379,448	Australia	275,774
Angola	237,947	France	271,896
DRC	211,060	United States	242,340
Mauritius	151,340	Portugal	233,904
Madagascar	133,807	Canada	132,553
Tanzania	121,466	New Zealand	66,283
Mozambique	85,023	Netherlands	30,071
Zambia	73,817	Germany	29,612
Malawi	21,634		
Seychelles	10,219		
Namibia	7,133		
Botswana	6,514		
Swaziland	3,440		
Lesotho	1,569		

TABLE 9: MAJOR DIASPORA CORRIDORS, 2015

Diaspora Corridor	No.
South Africa-UK	218,732
South Africa-Australia	183,370
Angola-Portugal	151,273
Zimbabwe-UK	132,942
Madagascar-France	120,400
South Africa-US	88,907
DRC-France	76,723
Mozambique-Portugal	67,991
Zimbabwe-US	50,001
South Africa-Canada	47,182

HARNESSING MIGRATION FOR DEVELOPMENT

There is a large and varied international literature on the subject of harnessing migration for development and inclusive growth. Many of these possible areas of intervention have been debated at length in international forums such as the Global Forum on Migration and Development (GFMD).[30] Rather than providing a comprehensive overview of all aspects of the migration and development nexus, here we focus only on those that provide particularly promising opportunities for programming in Southern Africa. The information and discussion that follows provides a background to the recommendations in Section 5.

Gender and Migration

Southern Africa is generally seen as a region undergoing rapid feminization of migration with female migrants increasing in numbers and as a proportion of the total.[31] Migrant stock data confirms the first observation but not the second (Table 10). Between 1990 and 2015, the number of female migrants in the SADC increased by several hundred thousand to 2.25 million. However, the proportion of female migrants actually declined over the same period from 46% to 43% of the total and the proportion of male migrants increased from 54% to 57%. In the major destination country (South Africa), the proportion of female migrants increased marginally from 38% to 40% but migration remained male-dominated (with 60% of the migrant stock being male). In 1990, there were more male than female migrants in 11 SADC countries; in

TABLE 10: PROPORTION OF MALE AND FEMALE MIGRANTS

	1990		2015	
	Female	**Male**	**Female**	**Male**
Angola	46	54	52	48
Botswana	40	60	45	55
DRC	50	50	45	55
Lesotho	48	52	46	54
Madagascar	44	56	43	57
Malawi	52	48	52	48
Mauritius	51	49	45	55
Mozambique	46	54	52	48
Namibia	47	53	46	54
Seychelles	41	59	30	70
South Africa	38	62	40	60
Swaziland	46	54	48	52
Tanzania	51	49	50	50
Zambia	49	51	50	50
Zimbabwe	44	56	43	57
Total	46	54	43	57

Source: United Nations Population Division (2015). Data retrieved on June 25, 2016 from http://www.un.org/en/development/desa/population/migration/data/

2015, the number was still 10 (with only Angola having shifted).

A second critical component of the feminization of migration is increased independent migration by women of all ages, educational backgrounds and skills levels. Unfortunately, with existing gender-neutral data sets, it is difficult to amplify this point. For example, South Africa's Department of Home Affairs releases data on the number of permanent and temporary residence permits granted each year, but this provides only country of origin and age breakdowns and not the sex of permit-holders. Given the employment, capital, education and skills criteria for most of the official residence and work permit categories in South Africa, we can reasonably assume a male bias in determining eligibility, meaning a likely male majority in legal residence and work-permit-holders. For obvious reasons, no accurate count or gender breakdown is available for informal migrants, who make up a significant but unknown proportion of total migrant numbers. There seems to be a persistent pattern of male domination in current refugee and asylum-seeker flows. In 2015, males represented 67% of the country's asylum claimants, females 33%.

There is limited gender-based data or analysis of migrant labour and employment, but the South African indications are that migrant women are more likely to be unemployed than migrant men. Data from the Quarterly Labour Force Survey for the third quarter of 2012 suggests that a migrant woman had only a 56% probability of being employed compared to a migrant man.[32] This requires further multivariate analysis by country of origin, migration category, date of arrival and geographical location for meaningful explanation beyond general gender discrimination.

Migrant Rights and Protections

Legal temporary work programmes are advocated internationally as a "triple development win" for countries of origin, countries of destination and migrants themselves.[33] Some countries, such as South Africa, have implemented bilateral temporary work programmes with other developing countries such as Cuba, Tunisia and India to import skilled migrants, especially in the health sector.[34] Mauritius has imported temporary workers from Bangladesh, India and China to work in construction and manufacturing.[35] Various countries have facilitated the temporary import of Chinese workers as part of major China-funded construction projects.[36] With the major exception of Mauritius, few Southern African countries have taken advantage of the opportunities created by temporary work programmes in the North.[37] These various bilateral temporary work initiatives, involving connections with other parts of the world, have not been systematically evaluated from the perspective of their positive or negative development impacts.

Within Southern Africa, the only significant temporary work programme (now in decline) is the contract labour system to the South African mines. Prior to 2002, the mining companies could recruit and employ as many foreign miners as they wished. This changed in 2002 with South Africa's new Immigration Act which obliged the mines to apply for new corporate permits to employ foreign migrants. This system proved cumbersome and the mines stopped employing new migrants from outside the country. Commercial farmers are thought to have been major users of the corporate permit system to legalize their employment of migrants but there is no information available on the corporate permit system.

There is a growing body of case-study evidence on informal temporary migration and the low wage regime and exploitative conditions in sectors such as construction, illicit mining, commercial agriculture and domestic work. For those migrant women who are employed, many are engaged in precarious livelihoods. Some are employed in potentially exploitative conditions with weak oversight or protection of their labour rights, for example as domestic workers[38] or farm workers.[39] Others are engaged in inherently precarious informal occupations such as trading, hair braiding and other beauty services, or craft production and sales, often conducted in unsafe spaces.[40] Related to their precarious working and living conditions, female migrants experience gender-based violence and other health vulnerabilities. This is particularly acute for those who engage in sex work: a 2010 survey of female sex workers in Johannesburg, Rustenburg and Cape Town found that 46% were migrants.[41]

Women and girls tend to be concentrated in the commercial, agriculture and domestic work sectors. It is clear that the poor treatment of regional migrants on the way to and at the workplace has an extremely negative impact on the migrants themselves and their households, but this is also antithetical to development and inclusive growth in their home countries. For example, low wages and other forms of financial extortion severely reduce the remitting ability of migrants. Employers of domestic and agricultural workers have been found to deny migrants their basic labour rights, engage in exploitative labour practices such as low pay, withholding wages, excessively long hours, poor accommodation and dangerous working conditions. Poor conditions and abuse at the workplace go unpunished when reporting to the authorities is likely to lead to arrest as an "illegal foreigner", job loss and deportation. Precarious employment in the agricultural and domestic service sectors is highly gendered with female migrants being most vulnerable to exploitation by formal and informal labour brokers and recruiters, employers and the police.

The potentially highly exploitative institutional mechanisms, both formal and informal, that connect employers to source areas for migrants are largely unknown and unregulated. As Kiwanuka et al conclude, "much more research is needed on the informal aspects of [women's] labour migration, which point to the presence of multiple dynamics and actors including locally based transnational networks of recruitment and migration, informal agencies and aspects of indebtedness."[42] Female migrant workers in commercial agriculture and domestic service face "nearly impossible barriers in accessing a legal right to work." This means that their legal situation is precarious and they are constantly vulnerable to arrest and deportation and to exploitation by employers that they are powerless to report and seek redress. The treatment of migrants travelling to and from places of work is largely unaddressed at a regional level (not just in South Africa), although the negative experiences of girl migrants in three countries have been identified by Save the Children.[43]

One of the major challenges confronting migrants is access to formal social protection programmes in countries of destination and, to a lesser degree, the portability of eligible social benefits across borders. Olivier has argued that "the constitutional and fundamental rights protection informing the social security position of intra-SADC migrants is weak and unsatisfactory."[44] Another study has highlighted the absence of good nationally representative data on migrant social protection and portability.[45] Much recent attention has been focused on the question of the portability of rights for migrant miners. Given the imminent demise of foreign migrant labour on the mines, however, the social protection challenge relates more to redressing the negative legacies of the system. Two legacies of mine migration are being addressed by various stakeholders:

- Unpaid social security benefits in the form of provident and pension funds amounting to over ZAR4.0 billion owed to at least 200,000 ex-mineworkers;[46] and

- The human and financial cost of the health burden on neighbouring countries from occupational disease.[47] In May 2016, the South African High Court allowed a class-action lawsuit against over 25 mining companies, which could eventually benefit as many as 300,000 ex-mineworkers with silicosis.[48]

Social security entitlements and compensation and the settlement of lawsuits could see significant sums being transferred from South Africa to impoverished ex-mineworkers and their families (Table 11).

TABLE 11: SOCIAL SECURITY BENEFITS OWED TO EX-MINEWORKERS

Social Security Institution	Amount	No. of Beneficiaries
Mineworkers Provident Fund	ZAR3,008,289,913	106,149
Living Hands Umbrella Trust	ZAR1,200,000,000	12,500
Mines 1970s Pension & Provident Funds	ZAR200,000,000	59,702
Sentinel Mining Industry Retirement Fund	ZAR101,000,000	Unknown
Compensation Commissioner for Occupational Diseases		18,000 (claims backlog) 274,000 (still to be compensated)
Compensation Fund		12,000 (still to be compensated)

Migration and Remittances

There is a considerable body of case-study research evidence to confirm that remitting is an extremely common practice in Southern Africa. However, much remitting is through informal channels, and accurate data on remittance flows at the regional level is not available. FinMark Trust observes that the "deficit of complete and high quality data" has made it difficult to formulate a comprehensive policy response.[49]

There are two main sources of data on overall cash remittance flows: (a) World Bank calculations and (b) FinMark Trust estimates. In this report, we relied on World Bank data, which provides a more comprehensive picture of bilateral flows across the region (Table 12):

- There has been a consistent increase in total global remittance flows to the countries of Southern Africa from USD200 million in 1995 to USD1 billion in 2014;

- The major remittance-sending countries in 2014 were South Africa (at USD639 million), Zimbabwe (USD50 million), Botswana (USD48 million), and Malawi and Mozambique (at USD31 million each);

- The major recipients were Zimbabwe (no data), Lesotho (USD426 million), Mozambique (USD128 million), Botswana (USD41 million), Tanzania (USD40 million), Zambia (USD37 million), Malawi (USD30 million) and Swaziland (USD23 million);

- The main remittance corridors are South Africa-Zimbabwe (no data), South Africa-Lesotho (USD414 million), South Africa-Mozambique (USD90 million), South Africa-Botswana (USD38 million) and Botswana-South Africa (USD33 million);

- Significantly, only a third (31%) of remittances to Southern African countries come from other countries within the region. Over two-thirds (69%) of remittances to

TABLE 12: REMITTANCE FLOWS WITHIN AND TO SOUTHERN AFRICA (USD MILLION)

	Total remittances sent	Total remittances received	Intra-regional remittances received	Extra-regional remittances received	Regional as percentage of total
Angola	6	11	5	6	45.4
Botswana	48	45	41	4	91.1
DRC	3	22	3	19	13.6
Lesotho	1	430	426	4	99.1
Madagascar	0	427	8	419	18.7
Malawi	35	38	30	8	78.9
Mauritius	1	249	15	235	6.0
Mozambique	35	161	128	33	79.5
Namibia	9	10	9	1	90.0
Seychelles	3	17	1	16	5.9
South Africa	639	866	91	775	10.5
Swaziland	12	24	23	1	95.8
Tanzania	15	389	40	349	10.3
Zambia	4	58	37	21	63.8
Zimbabwe	50	–	–	–	n/a
Regional total	861	2,747	857	1,890	31.2

Source: http://www.worldbank.org/en/topic/migrationremittancesdiasporaissues/brief/migration-remittances-data

Southern African countries therefore come from outside the region; and

- There are differences among countries in the proportion of remittances received from other countries in Southern Africa versus the proportion that comes from outside the region. In some countries, over 90% of remittances are intra-regional (Botswana, Lesotho, Namibia and Swaziland). In others, more than 80% of remittances come from outside the region (DRC, Seychelles, Mauritius, South Africa and Tanzania).

For purposes of harnessing remittances for development and inclusive growth, both sources of remittances need to be tapped.

Table 13 refers only to remittances through formal channels. It is well documented that the majority of migrants within the Southern African region use informal channels including personal conveyance. In some cases, especially Zimbabwe, there are specialist transporters of remittances who run small businesses in this sector. While increased use of formal channels is a desirable objective of banks and money transfer companies, and a fundamental aim of the World Bank, it needs to be established whether migrants use informal channels out of choice or necessity and what the impacts of formalization would be on informal operators, many of whom are themselves migrants.

One reason migrants may avoid formal channels is the cost of remitting in Southern Africa, among the highest globally. The global average cost of sending remittances was 7.5% of the amount received. In South Africa, the average was more than double the global average at 15.2%. Considerable work in reducing remittance costs has been done by FinMark Trust in trying to resolve what it calls the "problem of informalisation"; that is, the preference of remitters to utilize informal channels and the exclusionary practices of financial institutions.[50] Significant changes in the regulatory environment and technological advances now provide platforms for more efficient and cost-effective money transfer services, which may prompt a shift towards greater formalization and financial inclusion.[51]

In much of the discussion about remittances and development, the fact that migrants remit goods as well as cash is ignored. However, research suggests that this is an important aspect of remitting in Southern Africa. Just over one-third of the households in a five-country SAMP survey had also received goods in the previous year (Table 13).[52] Here again, there was considerable variation from country to country. Goods remittances were most important to households in Zimbabwe (68%) and Mozambique (65%) and least important to households in Lesotho (20%) and Swaziland (17%). Although the average annual value of cash remittances was about three times as much as goods remittances, in Mozambique they were almost the same and in Zimbabwe only twice as much. These figures suggest that goods remitting is a significant component of remitting in Southern Africa that needs more attention.

Globally, female migrants send approximately the same per capita amount of remittances as male migrants. Women tend to send a higher proportion of their income, even though they generally earn less than men.[53] They also usually send money more regularly and for longer periods of time. By sending smaller sums more often, women also tend to spend more on transfer fees. While men mostly remit to their partners, women often send remittances to the person (often another woman) taking care of her children to ensure that the money is spent on the children. Research by SAMP showed that many of these general patterns prevailed in Southern Africa with distinct gender differences in remitting amounts, frequency and means of remitting, remittance recipients and use of remittances. This evidence suggests that data, research and policy-making on migration needs to be gender-disaggregated.

Migration and Informal Entrepreneurship

The numbers of migrants running small and micro-enterprises or being employed in these businesses is considerable in towns and cities across the region. In South Africa, as many as one-third of migrants are self-employed in the informal economy. The Gauteng City-Region Observatory

TABLE 13: INTERNATIONAL AND INTERNAL GOODS REMITTING IN SOUTHERN AFRICA, 2008

	International migrants	Internal migrants
% receiving cash remittances	68	44
% receiving goods remittances	36	19
Mean cash remittances	ZAR4,821	ZAR5,434
Mean value of goods remittances	ZAR1,702	ZAR2,004
Importance to survival (%)	88	85
Source: SAMP		

(GCRO) Quality of Life Survey 2013 found that 11% of Johannesburg residents owned their own business and 65% of all business owners operated in the informal economy. Around 20% of informal business owners were migrants from another country.[54] The ILO definition of the informal economy encompasses precarious employment including those who are employed and self-employed in the informal sector and also those who are working unpaid in a household business and working in a job that does not entitle them to employment benefits. Under this definition, the proportion of migrants working in the informal economy rises to 53% in South Africa.[55] Recent case studies in South African cities provide various insights into the nature of informal self-employment.

Recent surveys of over 1,000 informal business owners in Cape Town and Johannesburg (Table 9) showed that:

- In both cities, 30% of those running informal enterprises were women;

- Many entrepreneurs were young (virtually all under the age of 50 and 70-80% under the age of 40);

- Informal migrant entrepreneurs come from a wide variety of countries inside and outside Southern Africa. The pattern was slightly different in the two cities: Zimbabweans predominated in both but Somalis and Ethiopians were more common in Cape Town than Johannesburg (23% versus 10%). On the other hand, entrepreneurs from Mozambique and Lesotho were more common in Johannesburg (19% versus 2%);

- The occupational distribution was similar in both cities with trade dominant in both (at around 60%); and

- The vast majority in both cities had a legal right to be in the country with only about 10% undocumented.[56]

Informal business owners are classified as self-employed but they also have positive development impacts in countries of destination and origin through (a) remittance of business profits to home countries; (b) generating employment in countries of destination for migrants and citizens. In Cape Town, for example, 30% of migrant-owned businesses employ other migrants while 41% employ South Africans;[57] (c) rental of business properties from local property owners; (d) providing cheaper services, including food, and credit to poor consumers in countries of operation; (e) supporting formal sector businesses and employment generation through purchase of products for resale from wholesalers and retailers; (f) payment of operating licences to municipalities; and (g) paying VAT on purchased goods.

The major challenges to business survival and expansion include (a) difficulties of securing start-up capital and consequent reliance on personal savings; (b) problems securing business loans from formal financial institutions, especially banks; (c) lack of basic business training and skills; (d) exclusion from the formal banking system and business banking, thus increasing vulnerability to crime; (e) direct competition from formal businesses especially supermarkets; (f) vulnerability to xenophobic attacks and destruction of stock and business premises; and (g) a hostile operating environment including official harassment, extortion and demands for bribes or protection money.

Diasporas for Development

As noted above, all of the countries of Southern Africa have sizable diasporas living outside the country. The African Union and many individual countries increasingly recognize the diaspora as an important actual and potential development resource for remittances, investments, philanthropy, tourism, training and skills transfer. While the SADC Secretariat has not articulated a policy for diaspora engagement at the regional level, many individual governments are developing plans and policies for diaspora engagement. An important information gap concerns the attitudes of diasporas themselves to engagement in development-related activities and initiatives in their countries of origin. There are four key questions: (a) what kinds of backward linkages, if any, do migrants maintain with their countries of origin? (b) what interest do they have in leveraging these linkages for development purposes? (c) what kinds of development-related activities are diasporas interested in and capable of initiating and supporting? and (d) are they prepared to work with governments and respond to government diaspora engagement policies or do they prefer to work outside government channels, for example with the private and NGO sectors?

Answers to these questions can only be gathered from research with diasporas. Two studies provide some insights for particular diasporas. The first is a study of the global Zambian diaspora undertaken by the IOM and the Diaspora Liaison Office of the Zambian Government in 2008 and updated in 2014.[58] The 2014 iteration reports the findings from 1,200 respondents:

- The primary reasons for leaving Zambia were employment/business opportunities (42%) and education (38%);

- As many as 70% left Zambia more than five years ago, 40% having been away for more than 10 years. Nearly

50% return to Zambia at least once per year. Only 9% have never returned since leaving;

- Around two-thirds (69%) intend to return to Zambia permanently while another 25% are unsure;

- The diaspora is highly skilled with around 70% having graduate degrees (including 40% with post-graduate degrees) and another 20% with college qualifications;

- Over 80% send remittances to Zambia, 44% on a monthly basis. Most send remittances to financially support family or friends (94%) and personal investment (37%). Remittances flow largely through formal channels (banks and money transfer companies);

- As many as 91% are interested in making private investments in Zambia, with the greatest sectoral interest in agriculture/horticulture (47%), import (28%), manufacturing (28%), tourism (26%) and transport (24%); and

- Nearly 60% express interest in contributing to or donating to development projects in Zambia, with only 11% uninterested. The preferred project areas include education (62%), healthcare (41%), infrastructure development (31%), childcare (26%) and microfinance initiatives (23%). Over 80% are interested in skills transfer and 41% in making financial contributions.

The second study by SAMP surveyed 2,450 migrants from SADC countries who had immigrated to Canada:[59]

- Only 19% of the sample entered Canada in the economic class. The bulk of the remainder entered as asylum-seekers/refugees (34%), students (18%) and family-class immigrants (15%). Irrespective of the category of entry, 53% had acquired Canadian citizenship;

- The immigrants had attained high levels of education before coming to Canada. For example, 30% had at least a university degree upon entry. As many as a third had to re-certify or retrain in Canada in order to work in a field for which they were already trained;

- The most common occupations included sales and service, health and finance, business and banking; and

- Almost two-thirds (62%) felt that they have an important role to play in developing their countries of origin. Only 15% said they had no role to play;

- Nearly 70% remit money to their country of origin. One-quarter remit at least once a month, another third at least once a year and the rest occasionally. The average amount remitted is CAD1,000 per year. Remitting largely consists of private funds sent to immediate and extended family. Nearly all remitters (95%) send money to immediate family members, while 10% send remittances to community groups and organizations;

- In terms of diaspora engagement activities, nearly 50% have participated in some kind of economic activity in their country of origin: 25% have exported Canadian goods for sale, 11% have invested in business, 11% have generated employment, and 10% have engaged in research partnerships. In terms of willingness to be engaged in the future, only nine percent said they had no interest; and

- The preferred avenues of engagement included skills transfer (mentioned by 58%), investing in businesses (55%), participation in development projects (52%), educational exchanges (52%), volunteer work (48%), fundraising for development projects (46%), philanthropy (42%), export and import of goods to and from the country of origin (38%), investing in infrastructural development (39%) and providing distance learning (37%). Others specifically mentioned their desire to be involved in activities that would lead to greater empowerment for women and children.

A related study of South African philanthropists in Canada found (a) that they preferred to work with non-governmental organizations in the education and health sectors; and (b) that some were generous givers but preferred to donate to Canadian causes, citing corruption and related reasons for not donating to South Africa.[60]

In sum, the research suggests that migrants from the Southern African region have not turned their backs on their countries of origin and that there is considerable latent potential for diaspora engagement in development-related activities in the region.

CHAPTER 4: MIGRATION AND DEVELOPMENT AS A REGIONAL CHALLENGE IN SOUTHERN AFRICA

INTRODUCTION

In principle, there is significant awareness among SADC member states about the need to strengthen efforts aimed at harnessing migration for inclusive growth and development. The member states of the SADC have more than a decade of participation in international and regional forums on migration and development (including the annual Global Forum on Migration and Development, the two UN High Level Dialogues on International Migration and the 2013 Diaspora Ministerial Conference) as well as the Migration Dialogue for Southern Africa (MIDSA) regional consultative process.[61] Many states should be cognizant of the key modalities and actions required to make migration work for development. The relationship between migration and development is also clearly articulated in the AU Migration Policy Framework and the African Common Position on Migration and Development. On the face of it, therefore, there are reasons to be optimistic about a regional migration and development agenda co-ordinated by the SADC Secretariat and implemented by member states.

In practice, little progress has been made on mainstreaming migration and development at the national or regional policy level. Regional efforts to forge a common approach to migration appear promising, but while states appear willing to make initial commitments to agreements, instruments and initiatives, they are generally unwilling to ratify and implement anything that appears to infringe on their national sovereignty or the interests of citizens.

This section of the report first examines the extent to which migration is recognized as a regional development issue. Section 4.2 presents the results of the NVIVO analysis of stakeholder interviews to assess the extent to which migration is seen as a regional issue and force for development. Section 4.3 discusses the limited success of initiatives to advance a common regional migration agenda by the SADC Secretariat. Section 4.4 provides a gender analysis of these regional initiatives. Section 4.5 examines other regional governance initiatives, including the Migration Dialogue for Southern Africa (MIDSA) process. Section 4.6 identifies various obstacles to a regional migration management approach in Southern Africa and highlights the importance of actions at the national level. Finally, and in that context, Section 4.7 examines the proposed new approach by South Africa to migration management and whether this signifies a new sensitivity to regional migration realities.

PERCEPTIONS OF MIGRATION AS A REGIONAL DEVELOPMENT ISSUE

There was a considerable degree of unanimity among the 80 stakeholders interviewed for this study on the importance of seeing migration as a development issue requiring a co-ordinated regional response in Southern Africa. There was some expectation of a difference in opinion between regional and national stakeholders. However, many of the latter were also willing to acknowledge that migration was not only an issue of national importance. Where they differed was on who should be driving the agenda: national governments or regional bodies. The main points of consensus among stakeholders were the following:

- There is a pressing need for a regional approach to migration and development in the SADC. The challenge is implementation;

- Migration within and to the SADC region is beneficial for economic development, poverty reduction and inclusive economic growth. Migration is a means of "levelling development" and reducing economic disparities;

- Migration to and from a country and within the SADC is an asset for the development of the regional economy, for poverty reduction and for inclusive economic growth. However, there is a need for proper planning and management of migration in the region in order to optimize the benefits;

- Increased development in the region will not necessarily reduce migration but could change migration patterns. It could reduce the economic reasons for migration and therefore mean less movement of unskilled labour. But there may be an increase in migration of skilled labour who believe they have better opportunities elsewhere;

- The criminalization of migration and not offering a legal route for migrants are challenges that need to be addressed. Greater freedom of movement of migrants for work or other economic activity within Southern Africa would be beneficial;

- The free movement of migrants is essential but most states reject it as infringing on their sovereign rights;

- A number of respondents felt that national governments should be driving the migration and development agenda in the region and that it was important to move from the security focus towards an economic and development focus. However, those with a more regional brief said that the SADC should drive the agenda even though the regional body was described by some as ineffective; and

- Most respondents knew about some of the AU and regional protocols and agreements but none were familiar with all.

MIGRATION INITIATIVES AND THE SADC SECRETARIAT

Freedom of Movement

At the regional level, there is a paucity of instruments that focus directly on migration and development. An evaluation of the SADC Regional Indicative Strategic Development Plan (RISDP) concluded that: "It is disconcerting that the relationship between migration and poverty is under-represented in the plan's proposed intervention areas and only addressed in a partial and circumscribed manner."[62]

Freedom of intra-regional movement has been a principle of SADC since its foundation, although this is not explicitly tied to positive development outcomes. Article 5(2)(d) of the SADC Treaty (1992) states that the SADC shall "develop policies aimed at progressive elimination of obstacles to the free movement of capital and labour, goods and services, and of the people of the region generally, among Member States." Despite this objective, unfettered free movement is very far from being a reality. The Secretariat has had no success in getting all member states to ratify its two major regional mobility policy initiatives:

- The 1995 Draft Protocol on the Free Movement of Persons provided for members of one state to freely enter, establish themselves and work in another state. The Protocol was abandoned in 1998 after major opposition from South Africa, Botswana and Namibia;[63] and

- The 2005 Draft Protocol on the Facilitation of Movement of Persons had similar provisions regarding visa-free entry, residence and establishment, but affirmed that migration management was a national competency. While calling for the harmonization of migration policies and legislation, it did not propose an over-arching regional migration policy and legislative framework. Instead, much of the protocol focuses on enhancing the

capacities of states to individually and collectively regulate migration and strengthen border management. The Protocol was tabled in 2005 but by 2016 only six states (Botswana, Lesotho, Mozambique, South Africa, Swaziland and Zambia) had ratified it, short of the 10 required for it to enter into force.

The trumping of regional mobility initiatives by national immigration policies focused on movement control is clear to experts: "The non-ratification and enforcement of the SADC Facilitation Protocol, a much less ambitious objective than its free movement predecessor, raises questions about the region and its Member States' political will and commitment to migration governance."[64]

SADC member states prefer to act bilaterally in their dealings with each other on migration. This emphasis began in the 1960s and 1970s (and the 1920s in the case of Mozambique and South Africa) when South Africa and its neighbours concluded bilateral treaties to regulate and monitor the supply of migrant mineworkers to the South African mines. These agreements have never been officially repealed but are outdated and largely defunct. Since 2000, South Africa and neighbouring states have pursued new bilateral approaches (including on migration) through Joint Permanent Commissions (JPCs) and Memoranda of Understanding.[65] The JPCs have facilitated some migration-related issues on a bilateral basis (visa waivers, for example) but they do not have explicit development-related goals. Further, it might be argued that if two states can achieve their basic goal of achieving greater control over migration through bilateral agreements, this acts as a further disincentive to implement multilateral instruments.

At the level of individual member states, the mandate and expertise required for, and resources devoted to, migration management is often limited to routine and operational capacity requirements, as opposed to a more strategic approach in which migration management is an essential component of the development objectives of a particular state. An audit of Poverty Reduction Strategy Plans (PRSPs), for example, found that "the knowledge base on migration and development that does exist is weakly incorporated into poverty policy in the region."[66] The South African National Development Plan 2030 admits that "South Africa, like most other African countries, has done little to increase the benefits of migration or reduce the risks migrants face."[67]

Little discernible progress has therefore been made with regard to the implementation of a free movement regime by the SADC Secretariat. In part, this is because there is very little data or analysis on the impact that removing border controls in the region would actually have. It is arguable that SADC is already a de facto free movement zone and that the removal of controls would not have a dramatic impact on migration flows. What it would do is provide legal channels for those who want to migrate, reduce the opportunities for personal enrichment by corrupt state functionaries on both sides of borders, eliminate current high levels of corruption and abuse in the immigration system, and reduce the exploitation of migrants who enjoy few rights and protections. However, free movement is likely to remain politically unpalatable to most states for the foreseeable future. Greater opportunities for legal and regulated migration may therefore be the best way forward in the short and medium term.[68]

Migrant Rights and Protections

One of the key components of inclusive growth strategies is poverty reduction through productive and decent employment. Given the high levels of poverty and inequality throughout Southern Africa, it is important to view migrant employment rights as an integral part of the inclusive growth agenda. Our recent study for UNRISD examined the issue of migrant protection and rights in the Southern African region as a whole and identified the various regional-level commitments to protecting migrant rights and the obstacles to their implementation:[69]

- The core international legal instrument with the potential to protect migrants in the region is the 1990 UN International Convention on the Protection of the Rights of All Migrant Workers and Members of Their Families (ICRMW). However, only Lesotho, Madagascar, Mozambique and Seychelles are signatories to the ICRMW. In Southern Africa, as is the case globally, there is considerable resistance to this Convention;[70]

- Within the SADC, member states are committed to upholding fundamental human rights including employment rights as per the SADC Charter on Fundamental Social Rights. However, nowhere in the Charter are migrants mentioned explicitly and no provision is made for the portability of rights and protections across state borders;

- The 2008 Code on Social Security deals with migrants, foreign workers and refugees in Article 17, and explicitly states that member states should progressively reduce migration controls, that all legally employed migrants are entitled to the same social security as citizens, and that "illegal migrants" should enjoy "basic minimum protection." The Code therefore acknowledges that the rights of migrants require attention but its non-binding character makes implementation problematic;

- All of the SADC member states have now ratified some of the core ILO Conventions dealing with labour rights (87, 100, 111 and 182). However, there are very low ratification rates of others. For example, only three states have ratified the employment policy and occupational safety and health conventions and just two states (Mauritius and South Africa) have ratified the 2011 Domestic Workers Convention. An assessment is needed of the implementation of ratified conventions as they pertain to migrant rights and the reasons for the low rates of ratification of others, including those affecting key migrant work sectors;

- The SADC Protocol on Employment and Labour was signed by Labour Ministers from all member states in 2014.[71] Article 19 deals with Labour Migration and Migrant Workers and contains several rights-based provisions, stating that member states will *endeavour* to: (a) strengthen mechanisms to combat smuggling and human trafficking; (b) ensure that fundamental rights are accorded to non-citizens, in particular labour/employment and social protection rights; (c) adopt measures to provide for the special needs of migrant women, children and youth; (d) adopt a regional migration policy in accordance with international conventions to ensure the protection of the rights of migrants; and (e) adopt measures to facilitate the co-ordination and portability of social security benefits for migrants. Two-thirds of the SADC member states need to ratify the Protocol for it to come into force but as of mid-2016 no states had done so. This prompted the SADC Labour Ministers to direct the SADC Secretariat, with the support of the ILO, to conduct a study to establish the problems underlying the non-ratification of the Protocol and explore ways to promote its ratification by member states. As with the Facilitation of Movement Protocol, the Employment and Labour Protocol may well remain an aspirational document with little concrete implementation; and

- The 2014 SADC Regional Labour Migration Policy Framework has as one of its four main aims to "strengthen protection of the rights of migrant workers."[72] Member states are enjoined to *strive* to put in place by 2019 a national migration policy that includes explicit rights-based objectives. The extensive list of rights for migrants contains two notable features: (a) it applies primarily to migrant workers in formal employment and not to undocumented, irregular or unregulated migrant workers; and (b) it appears to apply mainly to migrants in employment and not self-employment. Apart from its non-binding character, there are several rights (especially concerning equal access and opportunity with nationals) that member states are unlikely to implement.

In sum, the SADC Secretariat has made various efforts to put in place instruments that commit member states to protecting the rights of migrant workers. In practice, ratification and implementation are proving problematical as few member states are willing to ratify the appropriate instruments.

SADC Decent Work Programme

A current SADC initiative, in collaboration with the ILO, is the SADC Decent Work Programme (DWP), which runs from 2013 to 2019.[73] Although targeted at work and labour in general, the DWP does explicitly address migration and supports the principle of freer movement in the region. It identifies a "decent work deficit" as a motive for intra-regional migration and emphasizes that "all core international labour standards apply to all workers regardless of their nationality or immigration status, unless otherwise stated." The DWP recognizes that increasing numbers of migrants in the region are women and has a specific section on gender that urges strengthened commitment to existing SADC gender policies and protocols. It calls on SADC states to ratify and implement existing ILO Conventions and observes that most SADC member states have not yet ratified either the ICRMW or the ILO Domestic Workers Convention. It includes as a planned output a SADC Protocol to Eliminate Human Trafficking. Achievement of the DWP's objectives, including ratification and implementation of the various ILO and UN Conventions (especially the Domestic Workers Convention) along with the proposed anti-trafficking Protocol, could benefit migrants in the region.

Strengthening Institutional Mechanisms for Migration Management

The European Union (EU) recently funded a project to strengthen the capacity of regional integration institutions and organizations including the SADC, COMESA, IOC and EAC in collaboration with the EU Delegation in Botswana with three components: (a) monitoring of migration flows; (b) addressing labour migration flows within Southern Africa; and (c) addressing mixed migration flows into the Southern Africa region. The first component is designed to co-ordinate the collection of reliable data and statistics and research for monitoring migration and border security concerns. The main activities will include strengthening regional capacity for data collection, analysis and use, including through migration profiles, to better inform national and regional policies; standardizing migrant stocks and flows data collection within member states; establishing a formal data collection and exchange mechanism modelled on the European example; integrating migration modules in labour market surveys; and research, monitoring and evaluation on irregular migration, smuggling, trafficking and IDPs.

The second component is designed to co-ordinate South-South labour mobility through targeted regional policies and programmes, and standardized frameworks, mechanisms and tools. This component is motivated by the need for an overall regional policy framework to govern labour migration and harness the benefits of migration for sending, transit and receiving countries. Proposed activities including mapping regulatory frameworks for illegal employment and informal work, with emphasis on migrant protection; consensus-building on regional migration policy priorities and harmonising operational procedures; harmonizing national labour and employment legislation on the rights of migrants and aligning this to regional treaties, protocols, the ILO conventions and the AU Migration Framework; mainstreaming migration in the regional integration agendas of the economic communities; raising public awareness on migrant rights; and educating and providing protection to abused migrant workers.

The third component is directed at strengthening migration management through policies and programmes on irregular migration, smuggling of migrants and trafficking in migrants, refugees and internally displaced people (IDPs). As well as strengthening migration management, this component is designed to strengthen law enforcement to develop and implement regional policies on trafficking; develop regional and national policies to address smuggling of migrants and unaccompanied children; develop a regional framework to manage asylum-seekers, refugees and IDPs; and develop a regional framework for addressing disaster-induced displacement and migration.

GENDER ANALYSIS OF REGIONAL INITIATIVES

A gender analysis of the various AU and SADC strategic instruments shows that gender and migration issues do feature, albeit in piecemeal fashion:

- Gender is paid explicit attention within the AU Migration Framework: first, within the section on Labour Migration; second, as an emphasis within the section on Migrant Smuggling; third, as a category of vulnerable persons in the section on Forced Migration; and, finally, in a separate sub-section on Migration and Gender under "Other Social Issues". The AU Framework refers to a number of UN and ILO Conventions and Protocols, including the ICRMW and Domestic Workers Convention, urging their ratification and adoption by member states. The sections on gender point to the growing feminization of migration, including for labour in the care sector, but place greater emphasis on the vulnerability of female migrants to exploitation, trafficking and sexual slavery. Similar observations on the growing feminization of African migration and exploitation of female migrants are evident in the 2006 African Common Position on Migration and Development. Women migrants would benefit from the rights, protections and promotion of freer migration that are set out in the AU Framework and African Common Position. Yet these AU recommendations, while important and desirable as goals, are weakened by being non-binding and deferring to national laws and policies;

- The AU's Labour Migration Governance for Development and Integration in Africa (Joint Labour Migration Programme, or JLMP) was developed by the AU Commission in conjunction with the ILO, IOM and UNECA. This was formally adopted at the African Union Assembly in 2015. Among the key features of African migration identified in the JLMP is the increased feminization of labour mobility within and from the continent. Its recommendations include enhanced collection and analysis of gender disaggregated data on migrants' "economic activity, employment, skills, education, working conditions, and social protection." It also references the AU Labour and Social Affairs Commission's 2013 Youth and Women Employment Pact that includes the "promotion of regional and sub-regional labour mobility" as one of its goals;

- The SADC's Charter of Fundamental Social Rights (2003) refers explicitly to the UN Universal Declaration on Human Rights, African Charter on Human and People's Rights and ILO Constitution, but is couched largely in the language of workers' rights. It contains no express provisions dealing with the social rights of migrants as a category. Gender rights of "equality between men and women" are expressed in terms of employment, remuneration, equal opportunities and the right to reconcile occupational and family obligations. Given the informal nature of many female migrants' livelihoods, formal labour protection instruments may have limited impact in practice. The Social Charter is also weakly enforced;

- Article 19 of the SADC 2014 Protocol on Employment and Labour includes a clause "to adopt measures to provide for the special needs of women, children and youth". Article 20 calls for the promotion of productivity, decent work and rights protection in the informal sector, which is of particular significance for migrant women.

The Employment and Labour Protocol references other instruments, such as the 2008 SADC Protocol on Gender and Development, and includes gender equity and equality as specific objectives. However, the Protocol's commitments on paper would need to be turned into effective national laws and policies and practical local interventions if they are to become meaningful tools to protect migrant women's rights and support their economic contributions;

- The 2007 Code on Social Security aims at the co-ordination, convergence and harmonization of social security provisions and laws in SADC member states. Article 13 of the Code deals with "Gender" and Article 17 with "Migrants, Foreign Workers and Refugees". The gender provisions in the Code include equal access to social security by men and women, gender sensitization in the social security system, abolition of discriminatory laws and practices, and strategies for the eradication of poverty and economic empowerment of women. Provisions for migrants are expressed in terms of different migrant categories. In addition to urging states to work towards regional free movement of persons, the Code holds that *legal* migrants should enjoy equal treatment alongside citizens in social security systems and that states should facilitate the portability of benefits across borders. Combined, the Code's gender and migrant provisions should in theory provide a framework for female migrants' access to social security, but the reality is that state-provided social security is limited in most SADC member states even for citizens;

- Remarkably, for a document that is otherwise so broad-ranging, including reference to a suite of international Conventions and Charters, the 2008 Protocol on Gender and Development almost entirely omits reference to migration. There is reference to "human trafficking, especially of women and children." Along with the anti-trafficking provision, the Gender Protocol does include recommendations for adequate remuneration and protection of agricultural and domestic workers and recognition of women's contribution in the informal sector. These could be interpreted as potentially beneficial to migrant women in those occupational categories, especially when read in conjunction with the 2014 Employment and Labour Protocol; and

- Most of the rights and protections in the SADC's 2014 Labour Migration Policy Framework are expressed in gender-neutral terms of migrant workers and their families, but there are express provisions to "harness positive gender considerations and demographic dividends" of labour migration, along with elimination of discrimination and abolition of forced and child labour. As formulated and adopted, the Framework stands to benefit all migrant workers, although its emphasis on formal employment makes it potentially less applicable to women migrants. Its effectiveness, moreover, depends on its recommendations being actively adopted and implemented by national governments.

In sum, there are challenges in advancing gender-sensitive, rights-based migration governance in the SADC region. The scale, complexity and diversity of migration, combined with incomplete and inconsistent data, certainly make it difficult to measure and monitor the gender composition of migrant flows and stocks, or to understand the particular contributions and vulnerabilities of female migrants.

Regional-level instruments, polices and protocols do exist, but these are barely enforced and national laws and institutions take precedence. The persistent limitations of migration governance on the continent have been recognized as an obstacle to regional and continental poverty reduction by the African Development Bank in a report that also points to the vulnerability and marginalization of female migrants.[74] Furthermore, policies and instruments to protect migrant and gender rights are implemented within a difficult social and political context in which xenophobic and patriarchal attitudes persist.

Overall, SADC and AU policies and protocols on migration tend to emphasize the vulnerability of female migrants, rather than their role as active economic actors and contributors to development. A recent Overseas Development Institute (ODI) briefing on women and migration concludes that "[f]or women and girls to benefit from mobility, policies must support the empowerment and economic benefits of migration and also increase protection of female migrants."[75] This dual focus on empowerment and protection should guide programming and policy development on gender and migration in the region.

MIGRATION DIALOGUE FOR SOUTHERN AFRICA (MIDSA)

Migration Dialogue for Southern Africa (MIDSA) has become the forum that most clearly articulates the relationship between migration and development in regional and national policy discussions and tends to drive the regional migration and development debate within the SADC.[76] MIDSA is one of several global and African Regional Consultative Processes (RCPs) on migration that have emerged since the mid-1990s. These are informal, non-binding, interstate forums for dialogue on migration matters of mutual interest.[77] MIDSA was founded in Mbabane, Swaziland, in

November 2000 and convened regular inter-governmental forums attended by senior bureaucrats from Departments of Immigration and Home Affairs in member states (as well as other ministries on an ad hoc basis).[78] In 2010, MIDSA was scaled up to ministerial level with a conference in Windhoek on Managing Migration through Regional Co-operation.[79] A second Inter-Ministerial Conference was convened in Maputo, Mozambique, in 2013 on Enhancing Labour Migration in the SADC Region and a third in Victoria Falls, Zimbabwe, in 2015 on Addressing Mixed and Irregular Migration in the SADC Region: Protection of the Unaccompanied Migrant Child.

In 2012, MIDSA developed a Regional Roadmap on Enhancing Intra-Regional Migration for Sustainable Development. The roadmap was subsequently revised and endorsed as an Action Plan at the MIDSA Ministerial in Maputo in 2013. The Action Plan is non-binding and there is some overlap between its recommendations and those of the SADC Labour Migration Policy Framework and Article 19 of the Protocol on Employment and Labour. However, it also covers a range of other development-related areas that are absent from the SADC instruments. The current plan is that governments will annually report progress in achieving the goals of the MIDSA Action Plan.[80]

As acknowledged by the senior officials and Ministers who participate in MIDSA, it is precisely the informal, non-binding and consultative nature of the process that makes it possible to develop recommendations that would not have been made if they were to be binding on participating states. This does not mean that these conclusions and recommendations are of no value – on the contrary, it is because MIDSA acts as an awareness-raising "clearing house" that formal processes on migration and development within the SADC, and even at national level, might be able to advance at a more rapid pace in future. The SADC Secretariat has been a regular participant in MIDSA, although the relationship has remained informal. In 2013, as part of a sustainability strategy, member states agreed that MIDSA should be incorporated into formal SADC structures and processes, though this has yet to take place. There are questions about whether and when this should happen, and whether it could negate the value of the MIDSA process in driving the debate about migration and development in the region.

Unlike other RCPs, MIDSA has relied on donors for funding its activities without financial contributions from member states. This outside funding is of a short-term nature. While the IOM plays a strong leadership and organizational role, it does not guarantee the MIDSA's sustainability. While there is a significant international literature endorsing the value of RCPs in building regional co-operation on migration, there has been no systematic evaluation of the achievements and impact of MIDSA in its 16 years of operation. Until this has been undertaken, results-based donors and member states may be reluctant to commit the resources to sustain MIDSA's goal of advancing a development agenda around migration in Southern Africa.

CHALLENGES FACING A REGIONAL RESPONSE

Stakeholder Perceptions of Challenges

The stakeholder interviews elicited a wide range of opinions on the obstacles to a regionally co-ordinated and harmonized response to harnessing regional migration for development and inclusive growth. The results of the NVIVO analysis of responses are summarized below:

- The main obstacle to a regional response is the high level of economic disparity between SADC member states. This has led to a level of protectionism among the economically stronger states. High poverty levels within SADC countries are also an obstacle to a regional response. Addressing the issue of inequality and poverty on a national level is prioritized by governments, thus deflecting their focus from regional to domestic issues;

- Another major obstacle to the implementation of SADC regional migration policies and agreements is a lack of political commitment at the national level. Other obstacles to implementation are lack of data and information and lack of capacity of government officials. SADC countries overcommit to international issues and do not have the apparatus to manage regional agreements;

- Other challenges of implementing a regional approach include limited funding for tackling migration and development issues at the regional level; no regional or strategic plans; limited information and interest by member states to focus on migration as a regional issue; limited implementation of various protocols and lack of enforcement mechanisms; and different administrative systems in place in each member state;

- Xenophobia is a major obstacle to a regional approach as migrants often become scapegoats for a lack of government delivery. In order to tackle the issue of xenophobia the following were mentioned: awareness raising; educating communities; creating understanding of the role of migration in labour development and national development in the country; training the media; and getting policy makers to understand the positive role of migration in development;

- Ideas about how the ratification of inter-governmental agreements and protocols might be fast-tracked include a SADC commission of government officials and experts to make recommendations and move forward as matter of urgency; to create a timeframe for ratification; and to implement advocacy workshops with parliamentarians to lobby the SADC heads of state for ratification of instruments. If a government feels that a protocol is not in line with its interests it will not fast-track it. To address this, there is a need for diplomacy and negotiation which should involve helping each country understand the value of migration and appreciate the benefits for their country of ratification and of creating an enabling environment for migrants;

- Harmonization of migration policies is a key goal. Harmonization of national policies in the SADC region is gradually occurring through the MIDSA process and the SADC Labour Migration Framework. However, unless governments integrate migration into national development plans and budget for this, it is impossible to expect implementation; and

- There is a gap in reliable data around migration with most people using estimates. The quality and availability of data for mapping migration flows and for understanding the impacts of migration on development is poor. Greater evidence production would enhance inter-governmental co-operation in terms of migration management.

Political Analysis of Challenges

- **Absence of Political Will:** This refers to the unwillingness of governments to commit to the development and implementation of specific regional policies and programmes. However, most of the existing agreements and protocols are signed at ministerial level. Thus, at least at the level of principled agreement, there does seem to be a degree of political will and a commitment to the less contentious regional instruments.

- **Lack of Capacity:** A significant reason for the slow progress in developing a cohesive set of policies and programmes aimed at harnessing the development benefits of migration, both at national and regional level, is the absence of properly mandated and resourced institutions. This is not limited to the SADC Secretariat or national governments – many of the civil society organizations involved in migration-related research or programmes are also constrained by lack of resources. The absence of knowledge and expertise, as well as technical, logistical and financial resources, provides a major impediment to both the development of appropriate policies and programmes and their implementation. Lack of capacity is a problem that needs to be addressed before significant progress in implementation can be made.

- **Overlapping Institutional Mandates:** Migration is often referred to as a cross-cutting issue, requiring a high level of co-operation and cohesiveness between government ministries and departments within national governments, which in turn needs to be replicated between governments at the regional scale. At the level of the SADC Secretariat, this "dilemma of jurisdiction" is reflected in the fact that while it is the custodian of the Protocol on the Facilitation of Movement of Persons, the actual development of migration-related policies and programmes is located elsewhere – in the case of labour migration, within the SADC Employment and Labour Sector. Ideally, and consistent with proposed approaches to mainstreaming migration in national development policies and programmes, the institutional mandate and authority to develop and implement such policies and programmes should be located in the highest office at the national level and at the level of the SADC within one part of the Secretariat, possibly the Directorate of Human Development and Special Programmes.

- **Disjuncture Between Regional and National Priorities:** The fact that many of the regional agreements are not reflected in national policies, legislation and programmes partly accounts for the slow progress because implementation largely depends on national governments allocating the necessary resources. This is often not done because regional migration priorities are not seen as consistent with national priorities. Many governments prefer to view migration in negative terms, as a threat to the interests of citizens and in need of control. In this respect they often echo the views of their constituents who want to see a reduction in migration, tighter controls, increased border controls, enforcement and deportations, and who exhibit very low levels of tolerance of migrants even from neighbouring countries. This inauspicious environment, in which the views of citizens and the actions of governments are mutually reinforcing, does not help national-level discussion about the development implications and value of regional migration.

- **Absence of Reliable Data and Information:** General migration patterns and dynamics are reasonably well documented but the development and inclusive growth impacts of migration for countries of origin and destination are less well understood, even among researchers. The need for data collection and research also has a

downstream function to assess the potential and outcome of alternative policy choices. Similar to lack of capacity, when lack of data is offered as a reason for slow progress, it is often dismissed as an excuse. However, it may in fact account for the lack of political commitment in some cases, since policymakers are unlikely to introduce new policies and programmes if they are uncertain about potential outcomes.

SOUTH AFRICA'S NEW MIGRATION PARADIGM

Basic Principles

South Africa's promised new migration paradigm was given policy substance by the gazetting of the Green Paper on International Migration in South Africa in Government Gazette No. 40088 on 24 June 2016. The drafting of the Green Paper represents the second major effort at overhauling South Africa's immigration policy. The first process began in 1997 when both a Green Paper and White Paper were published and ended when the Refugees Act of 1998 and the Immigration Act of 2002 were adopted (following which there were several amendments to both the legislation and the regulations, but no substantive redrafting). In many ways, the Green Paper represents a significant departure from the way in which migration is currently managed, not least because it begins to provide significant clarity in terms of policy vision and intent, even though there is still a substantial need for discussion and consultation.

The Green Paper displays a fundamental tension between existing control-oriented, securitized approaches to migration which start from the premise that migrants are a threat or risk to national sovereignty and a more optimistic view that migration can be harnessed for national interests. What these contrasting, and at times contradictory, positions share is the view that migration policy is fundamentally a matter of protecting national sovereignty and national self-interest. In this respect, the Green Paper advocates the need for a set of common goals and objectives around which migration policy can be developed and strategically managed to contribute towards the achievement of South Africa's national priorities, such as nation-building and social cohesion, inclusive economic growth and national security. At its heart, therefore, is the articulation and defence of national sovereignty and self-interest rather than any broader commitment to regional migration management, regional development and the realities of South Africa's dominant economic role in the region.

In looking towards the framing of a new set of policy parameters, the Green Paper sets out key principles for migration policy:

- South Africa has a sovereign right to manage international migration in its national interests;

- International migration policy must be oriented towards Africa;

- International migration policy must contribute towards nation-building and social cohesion;

- International migration policy must enable South Africans living abroad to contribute to national development priorities; and

- The efficient and secure management of migration is the responsibility of individual countries, all countries collectively and regional structures.

The most controversial proposals in the Green Paper relate to the country's refugee protection regime and policy proposals to make it far less welcoming of asylum-seekers and refugees. These proposals are based on the assumption that the existing system is overwhelmed by bogus asylum-seekers, a highly contentious argument given that it could equally be argued that South Africa's failure to develop a coherent response to the Zimbabwean crisis is the root cause of the phenomenon of asylum-seeking by economic migrants (a problem now largely overcome by the granting of amnesty to Zimbabweans). The associated argument is that the courts were wrong in granting asylum-seekers the right to work. By removing this right, and confining asylum-seekers to reception centres, it is assumed that the practice of asylum-seeking by economic migrants will cease. This, of course, completely ignores evidence of the positive economic contribution of refugees and asylum-seekers who, under existing law, are permitted to pursue economic livelihoods.

Here we focus on the policy proposals that have clear development-oriented motivations and intended outcomes.

Skills Migration

The Green Paper acknowledges that South Africa has critical skills shortages, that these gaps can be filled through immigration and that the country needs to compete on the global skills market. Much of this is consistent with current strategies, but as the GP correctly notes, the system is administratively inefficient and lacks flexibility. What is lacking, according to the GP, is an institutional arrangement that ensures that labour market information is analyzed and used

to make strategic decisions on the recruitment and retention of skills.

The Green Paper proposes (a) a points-based system as a means of transparent recruitment (something first proposed in the 1997 draft Green Paper and rejected by the then Minister of Home Affairs); (b) that desirable immigrants should be fast-tracked to permanent residence, a major departure from current policy that is fixated on temporary migration; and (c) South Africa should increase its skills pool by retaining students who have come to study in the country. Although acknowledging that this could lead to a loss of trained professionals for other African countries, and the SADC region, this is clearly trumped by national self-interest. Whether newly-minted graduates have the skills and experience to fill skills needs is, of course, questionable. In essence, since so many of South Africa's international students are from the SADC region, the proposed options for student retention are likely to advantage South Africa and disadvantage the region as a whole.

Diaspora Engagement

Unlike previous policy drafting exercises and proposals, the Green Paper includes and emphasizes the need for a proactive approach to engaging with South Africans in the diaspora. The proposal involves setting up a diaspora institution to consolidate and integrate existing initiatives, but also to expand engagement to include exchange programmes, investment, facilitating remittance transfers, and return and reintegration. The GP acknowledges that South Africa has no diaspora engagement policy nor an institutional mechanism for co-ordinating engagement. It notes that such institutions perform at least four functions: (a) promotion of emigration to meet varied national goals such as labour and investment; (b) exportation and student exchange programmes; (c) tapping into the resources of the diaspora – remittances, investment, tourism and the sharing of skills and knowledge; (d)?embracing diaspora communities through multinational citizenship, consular services, country ambassadors and re-integration programmes; and (d) reintegration of returnees.

The Green Paper proposes the establishment of a diaspora institution to (a) consolidate existing initiatives under a single multifaceted emigration strategy; (b) establish a formal and permanent mechanism to co-ordinate relevant government agencies and public policies relating to the needs of South African expatriates; (c) registration of South African expatriates and provision of consular services; (d) establishment of diaspora forums in countries with a high number of South African expatriates; (e) establishment of diaspora ambassadorial and knowledge networks; (f) provide ways in which emigrants can transfer skills back to South Africa, such as visiting lectureships and public and private sector partnerships; (g) incentive schemes that will motivate South African expatriates to invest in the country; (h) a reintegration programme for those who want to return home; and (i)?support mechanisms for those who want to emigrate for study and work purposes.

The idea that the diaspora is a potential development resource is a major departure from existing policy, as is the proposal to institutionalize diaspora engagement. However, as the GP notes, "further research in this area needs to be undertaken and to inform proposals for the creation of a South African diaspora institution."

Management of Regional Migration

The Green Paper constantly reiterates its African orientation. From a migration and development perspective, this section contains arguably one of the most important policy considerations for South Africa, and one that is significantly absent from the current policy as framed by the 1999 White Paper on International Migration. Locating the issue of migration within the broader context of regional integration, this section effectively proposes that migration is a key element both as a means towards, as well as an outcome of, integration and development in Africa.

Following an analysis of some of the existing instruments and initiatives pertaining to migration, the GP effectively commits South Africa to the development of a migration policy that supports the efforts of regional bodies to achieve higher levels of integration, which by implication means a commitment to free movement, or at least facilitating the movement of persons. Of particular relevance is the focus of the Green Paper on the management of economic migration from the SADC region to South Africa.

The Green Paper recognizes not only the historical reality of economic migration to South Africa from other SADC member states, but also argues that migration patterns are unlikely to change and that policy has to be responsive to this reality. Specifically, it recognizes the challenges related to low-skilled economic migration and puts forward potential policy options to be considered. In these options, the GP essentially takes a middle-of-the-road approach, noting the absence of regulated mechanisms for low-skilled economic migration while acknowledging the futility of trying to stop it.

On the other hand, the Green Paper acknowledges that free movement is not a reality and thus proposes a permitting regime that would facilitate the movement of low-skilled economic migrants and entrepreneurs from other SADC member states. These include a quota-based SADC special work visa, a SADC trader's visa and a SADC SME visa. In essence, these visas represent a special dispensation to low-skilled economic migrants from SADC, albeit with specific requirements and conditions. This is a significant departure from the current policy approach, which does not make provision for low-skilled economic migrants. This lack of provision, the Green Paper argues, results in higher levels of irregular migration and "strategic asylum-seeking".

The Green Paper argues that it would be easier to develop bilateral agreements with specific countries than attempting to develop multilateral agreements that, by definition, would take longer to conclude and implement.

This integrationist approach to migration policy represents a more welcoming and positive approach to low-skilled economic migrants from the SADC region but the Green Paper does not discuss the potential response from South Africans to such an approach and makes no proposals to mitigate potential negative reaction.

Development Implications

The focus on the need to harness the benefits of migration for development and, in particular, the emphasis on *"managing migration in the national interest"* suggests that there is a long-term policy view that no longer confines the management of migration to regulating the entry and exit of persons, but fundamentally links it to the aspirations, needs and developmental priorities of the country. Less articulated is a vision for South Africa's role in regional development or an assessment of what the implementation of policies animated by national interests might mean for other SADC countries.

That said, the Green Paper does recognize the need to link migration policy and management to the imperatives of continental and specifically SADC co-operation and integration. In this regard, the proposals pertaining to the special permits and other mechanisms for citizens of SADC member states and other African countries are particularly relevant. Regrettably, these proposals may prove to be the most controversial and difficult to implement, given the current public climate of hostility towards all migrants in South Africa. The GP does not specifically address the issue of official and public sentiments and attitudes towards migrants and migration in any substantive detail. Given that these policy proposals represent a significant departure from prevailing practice, the need for consensus-building around these proposals, focusing on a set of shared interests and outcomes, is critically important.

Gender and Migration

The Green Paper mostly treats economic and humanitarian migration streams as if they are gender-neutral flows of individuals bearing identifiable attributes or skills. Given the strongly gendered nature of the labour markets (skilled and unskilled) in which migrants do or will participate, the specific employment sectors and skills determinants by which prospective immigrants will be admitted will have different effects on men and women and produce gender-imbalanced migration streams. None of the data presented in the Statistical Profiles of International Migrants in the GP is broken down by gender. This makes it impossible to identify the gender composition of current migrant flows or how these change over time or vary by employment sector, visa category or country of origin. Collection and analysis of gender-disaggregated data should be undertaken to assess the impact of current policy and inform further policy development.

The absence of consideration of gender or sexual identity in the section on refugees and asylum-seekers is notable. The GP proposes substantial changes to the current refugee and asylum policy and practice. Considerable attention is given to the "safe third country" principle, and there is a proposal to establish asylum-seeker processing centres near South Africa's borders, where asylum-seekers would be accommodated while their applications are processed. Each of these measures, if implemented, raises concerns in terms of gender and sexual identity. Politically stable countries designated as "safe" may not be so for individuals seeking asylum on grounds of social rather than political persecution – for example, people who identify as LGBTQ. Asylum-seeker processing centres are likely to be difficult places in which to guarantee safety and protection for women, children and other vulnerable groups. The proposed restriction of the right of asylum-seekers to work removes an important survival strategy and may force women (and men) into practices that make them vulnerable to violence and exploitation, such as sex work.

No migration policy can be entirely gender-neutral in its outcome and impact. Furthermore, to ignore the gender dimensions of migration policy risks undermining both economic objectives and humanitarian obligations. It is important that gender considerations be incorporated in the next stages of policy development.

CHAPTER 5: OPTIONS AND ENTRY POINTS

INTRODUCTION

A regional migration programme for Southern Africa needs to be guided by, and contribute directly to, the implementation of various strategic regional instruments. This section therefore presents the results of an analysis of the provisions and recommendations of these regional and inter-regional strategic frameworks/agreements. All of the instruments contain specific recommendations for programming that could harness migration for development and inclusive growth. Section 5.2 develops a 10-point thematic programming framework (PF) based on the objectives and content of the instruments and then extracts and classifies specific recommendations from each instrument and incorporates them into the PF.

Section 5.3 then uses the PF to classify the existing regional migration-related programmes on which information was collected in the fieldwork and are currently being implemented or planned in Southern Africa. This analysis has three main purposes: (a) to identify areas already covered by existing programmes; (b) to identify gaps in current programme and/or areas that need strengthening; and (c) to identify the main stakeholders involved in regional migration for development and inclusive growth.

PRIORITY PROGRAMMING AREAS IDENTIFIED IN MIGRATION INSTRUMENTS

A major objective of this report is to relate potential programming for harnessing migration for development and inclusive growth to relevant continental and regional strategic instruments. A systematic approach to these instruments could assist in briefing all stakeholders about their objectives, content and relevance to migration in Southern Africa. The instruments reviewed include the following:

- 2016 Sustainable Development Goals (SDGs)

- 2015 Valetta Accord (VA)

- 2006 African Union Framework (AUF)

- 2006 African Common Position on Migration and Development (ACP)

- AU Joint Labour Migration Programme for Africa (JLMP)

TABLE 14: PROGRAMMING FRAMEWORK

Issue	Entry Points
Addressing the Relationship between Migration and Development	Mitigating Root Causes Mainstreaming Migration
Enhancing Regional Co-operation on Migration Management for Development	Facilitating Free Movement Harmonizing Policies and Frameworks Building Institutional Capacity
Promoting Decent Employment	Implementing Better Policies Guaranteeing Better Work Designing Temporary Programmes
Ensuring Rights and Protections for Migrants	Eliminating Exploitation Securing Social Protection Countering Xenophobia
Facilitating Skills Migration	Removing Barriers Recognizing Qualifications Retaining/Importing/Building Skills
Adding Value to Remittances	Improving Financial Literacy Reducing Remittance Costs Optimizing Remittance Uses
Incorporating Gender Dimensions of Migration	Promoting Awareness Supporting Female Migrants
Building Migrant Entrepreneurs	Entrepreneurial Support Cross-Border Trade
Engaging Diasporas	Building Linkages Encouraging Contributions
Creating a Knowledge Platform	Migration Data Collection Information Exchange Research Priorities Capacity-Building

- 2005 SADC Protocol on the Facilitation of Movement of Persons (SADC Facilitation)

- 2014 MIDSA Action Plan (MAP)

- SADC Labour Migration Policy Framework (SADC LMPF)

- SADC Protocol on Employment and Labour (SADC EL)

To classify the many recommendations and commitments in these instruments, and to identify areas common to each, we developed a programming framework (or PF) with 10 issues and related entry points. We then extracted any specific recommendations relating to harnessing migration for development in each instrument and allocated them to the appropriate issue and entry point.

TABLE 15: ANALYSIS OF RECOMMENDATIONS IN REGIONAL INSTRUMENTS

1. Addressing the Relationship between Migration and Development
Mitigating Root Causes
▪ Enhance employment opportunities and revenue-generating activities in regions of origin and transit of migrants, including through public and private investment in favour of agriculture and rural economy development (VA).
▪ Put in place strategies aimed at reducing poverty, improving living and working conditions, creating employment opportunities and developing skills that can contribute to addressing the root causes of migration (AUF).
▪ Acknowledge that productive investments can help to address some of the causes of migration, recognize the need to promote economic growth by fostering trade, productive investment and employment, and implement economic and social policies geared towards alleviating migration pressures (AUF).
Mainstreaming Migration
▪ Integrate migration in development and poverty eradication strategies and programmes, in particular in areas such as labour market/employment, private sector development, education, health, social protection and security (VA).
▪ Facilitate technical co-operation activities with international agencies and other concerned entities to enhance the developmental effects of labour migration (AUF).
▪ Encourage AU member states to integrate migration and development policies in their national development plans (AUF).
▪ Integrate migration and displacement issues into the national and regional agenda for security and stability in addition to development and co-operation (AUF).
▪ Include migration in the framework of development strategies and national and regional programming with the purpose of supporting the economic and social development of the regions from which migrants originate in order to address the root causes of migration and reduce poverty (AUF).
▪ Mainstream migration in national development plans (ACP).
▪ Conduct training workshops for participants from government, private sector, civil society and worker organizations on mainstreaming migration into national development policies (MIDSA).
▪ Strengthen regional integration and inclusive development (JLMP).

2. Enhancing Regional Co-operation on Migration Management for Development

Facilitating Free Movement

■ Step up efforts to promote legal migration and mobility within bilateral co-operation frameworks such as Mobility Partnerships and Common Agendas on Migration and Mobility (VA).

■ Enhance co-operation and co-ordination among states in sub-regions and regions with a view to facilitating free movement from which an Africa-wide framework on the free movement of persons should be developed (AUF).

■ Harmonize sub-regional migration policies to promote free movement and right of residence (AUF).

■ Ensure intra-African freedom of movement of migratory flows (ACP).

■ Achieve wider elaboration, adoption and implementation of harmonized free circulation regimes and coherent national labour migration policy in the regional economic communities (JLMP).

■ Facilitate the movement of persons in the SADC as a vehicle for achieving economic integration (SADC Movement).

Harmonizing Policies and Frameworks

■ Support continental, regional and sub-regional frameworks for mobility and migration (VA).

■ Develop a common migration policy among African countries towards harmonization of laws, standards, procedures, information, dis-semination and sharing, statistics, documents, and efficient use of resources (AUF).

■ Look for collective solutions to migration through bilateral, multilateral and regional agreements and dialogue in a manner that benefits all parties: origin country, destination country and migrants (AUF).

■ Develop national and regional migration policy frameworks to address national/regional migration issues (MAP).

■ Draft a template for common regional standard operating practices related to migration management (MAP).

■ Encourage the development of migration policies for member states that do not have a policy in place (MAP).

■ Harmonization of national labour and employment legislations on the rights of foreign workers aligning to various treaties, protocols and conventions (SADC LMPF).

■ Adoption of a common set of co-operation principles on labour migration (SADC LMPF).

■ Mapping and harmonization of legislation leading to the adoption of consistent policy frameworks at sub-regional level (SADC LMPF).

■ Ensure coherence between labour migration, employment policies and other development strategies within member states (SADC EL).

Building Institutional Capacity

■ Facilitate orderly, safe, regular and responsible migration and mobility of people, including through the implementation of planned and well-managed migration policies (SDG Target 10.7)

■ Set up national and sub-regional social dialogue mechanisms to address migrant labour issues (AUF).

■ Encourage regional consultative processes and dialogue on irregular migration to promote greater policy coherence at the national, sub-regional and regional levels (AUF).

■ Establish regional mechanisms for tripartite policy consultation and co-ordination on labour migration issues, and facilitate consultation and co-operation with other regions (JLMP).

■ Initiate dialogue with other Regional Co-operative Processes, such as EAC and COMESA, in order to discuss migration in an integrated manner and find solutions inter-regionally (MAP).

■ Design and implement a capacity-building training programme for government, civil society, private sector and worker organizations (MAP).

■ Create a SADC labour litigation mechanism (SADC LMPF).

■ Technical training and assistance to migration and labour ministries, unions and employers' organizations on migrant workers' rights, drawing on international, regional and SADC frameworks (SADC LMPF).

■ Strengthen labour inspectorates across SADC member states (SADC LMPF).

■ Create a legal and policy framework within the SADC through harmonized labour and social security legislation (SADC EL).

3. Promoting Decent Employment

Implementing Better Policies

■ Establish regular, transparent and comprehensive labour migration policies, legislation and structures at national and regional level (AUF).

■ Implement labour migration policies and legislation that incorporate appropriate labour standards to benefit labour migrants and members of their families (AUF).

■ Incorporate provisions from ILO Conventions 97 and 142 into policy (AUF).

■ Create transparent (open) and accountable labour recruitment and admissions systems based on clear legislative categories and harmonizing immigration policies with labour laws (AUF).

■ Strengthen governance and regulation of labour migration and mobility in Africa (JLMP).

■ Harmonize labour migration policy and legal frameworks (MAP).

■ Harmonize required documentation for SADC migrant workers employed within the region and without (SADC LMPF).

■ Harmonize visa requirements for work permits for SADC nationals and third-country nationals (SADC LMPF).

■ Harmonize pension and social security in both private and public schemes (MAP).

■ Harmonize fundamental rights of migrant workers (MAP).

■ Harmonize work-seekers' visa requirements for SADC nationals (SADC LMPF).

Guaranteeing Better Work

■ Protect labour rights and promote safe and secure working environments for all workers, including migrant workers, in particular women migrants, and those in precarious employment (SDG Target 8.8).

■ Incorporate mechanisms that monitor the provision of decent work for migrants and enable them to access legal provisions for social protection (AUF).

■ Provide social protection and social security benefits (particularly unemployment insurance, injury compensation and pensions) for labour migrants (AUF).

■ Ensure labour migrants experiencing job losses are adequately provided for or receive financial assistance for return and resettlement (AUF).

■ Enable better social and economic integration of migrants, effective labour and social protection mechanisms, and sustainable labour market systems (JLMP).

■ Support decent work for migrants with effective application of labour standards to migrant workers (JLMP).

■ Ensure migrant workers have access to social benefits, health services and continuum of care across borders (MAP).

■ Inform potential migrants, returning/seasonal migrants of their rights and of minimum standards, of possibilities to claim those rights and report abuses (SADC LMPF).

■ Educate migrant workers, labour representatives and employers regarding the implications of legal requirements (SADC LMPF).

Designing Temporary Programmes

■ Promote fair recruitment practices (VA).

4. Ensuring Rights and Protections for Migrants

Eliminating Exploitation

■ End abuse, exploitation, trafficking and all forms of violence and torture against children (SDG Target 16.2).

■ Take immediate and effective measures to eradicate forced labour, end modern slavery and human trafficking and secure the prohibition and elimination of the worst forms of child labour, including recruitment and use of child soldiers, and by 2025 end child labour in all its forms (SDG Target 8.7).

■ Strengthen the capacities of local authorities and civil society to advocate for and protect rights of migrants (VA).

■ Ensure effective implementation by relevant national authorities of existing legislation and measures against employers who exploit irregular migrants (VA).

■ Create an enabling environment for migrant rights to be respected including allowing migrants to defend their rights by forming migrant associations (AUF).

■ Ensure the respect of the dignity and the protection of the rights to which migrants are entitled under international law, especially the right to equal treatment (ACP).

■ Effectively provide protection to abused migrant workers by designing and implementing emergency plans in situations of gross rights abuses and safety infringements (SADC LMPF).

■ Harmonize regional labour migration policy in order to protect and guarantee equal rights and access to decent and productive work for migrant workers (MAP).

■ Adopt a regional migration policy to ensure the protection of the rights of migrants (SADC EL).

Securing Social Protection

■ Extend social security to migrants through access and portability regimes compatible with international standards and good practice (JLMP).

■ Harmonize legislation towards better inclusion of migrant workers into state-provided social services (SADC LMPF).

■ Harmonize and monitor the delivery of migrant workers' social rights in the private sector in the framework of a decent work agenda across the region (SADC LMPF).

■ Ensure that fundamental rights are accorded to non-citizens, in particular labour/employment and social protection rights (SADC Employment).

■ Establish an autonomous regional agency to address cross-cutting issues pertaining to social protection such as streamlining and facilitation of portability of social security benefits across borders, stipulating applicable regional minimum standards and regulating institutional mechanisms that guarantee relevant entitlements, rights and obligations across borders (SADC Employment).

Countering Xenophobia

■ Encourage the development and implementation of national and regional strategies or policies for integrating migrants into host societies and for counteracting xenophobia and discrimination (VA).

■ Promote respect for, and protection of, the rights of labour migrants including combatting discrimination and xenophobia (AUF).

■ Disseminate information about migrants, through public information and education campaigns and other means, to promote respect for, tolerance and understanding of migrants, and to counter anti-immigrant and xenophobic attitudes (AUF).

■ Implement the relevant elements from the Programme of Action of the World Conference Against Racism and Xenophobia, including measures to ensure the fair and non-discriminatory treatment of migrants, regardless of status, with particular attention to preventing discrimination against women and children (AUF).

5. Facilitating Skills Migration

Removing Barriers

■ Promote the mobility of students, researchers and entrepreneurs (VA).

■ Maximize the contribution of skilled professionals in the continent by facilitating mobility and deployment of professionals in a continental and regional framework (AUF).

■ Recognize the relevance of short-term migration and the movement of persons in the context of trade of services, stressing the need for more information on the movement of highly skilled workers and on the "trade value" of such moves (AUF).

■ Set up a dialogue between all government agencies dealing with migration, trade and labour issues in order to establish means of dealing with temporary movement of persons supplying services (AUF).

■ Encourage the movement of skilled African labour between the host countries and the countries of origin (ACP).

■ Create an environment conducive to circular migration (brain circulation) (ACP).

■ Relax entry requirements for service providers, ensuring non-discriminatory treatment in the terms and conditions of service, as well as elimination of the economic needs tests in recruitment (ACP).

■ Boost the growth of a regional skills pool based on facilitated circulation within the region and increased attractiveness (SADC LMPF).

■ Explore the scope for SADC multilateral and bilateral agreements to encourage circular migration of skilled personnel (e.g. twinning of medical schools and health care facilities) (SADC LMPF).

Recognizing Qualifications

■ Identify, as a pilot, one or more professions where participating states commit to making progress on facilitating recognition of skills and qualifications (VA).

■ Resolve skills shortages and skills-education mismatches while increasing recognition of harmonized qualifications (JLMP).

■ Establish the state of available skills regionally in critical sectors and an inventory of barriers to their circulation (SADC LMPF).

■ Establish the scope for standardization of skills recognition across the SADC (SADC LMPF).

Retaining/Importing/Building Skills

■ By 2020, substantially expand globally the number of scholarships available to developing countries, in particular least-developed countries, small island developing states and African countries, for enrolment in higher education, including vocational training and information and communications technology, technical, engineering and scientific programmes, in developed countries and other developing countries (SDG Target 4b).

■ Elaborate a framework for social and economic offsets from host countries to mitigate the effects of large-scale departures of highly skilled African professionals in critical sectors (ACP).

6. Adding Value to Remittances

Improving Financial Literacy

■ Support financial education and inclusion of migrants and their families (VA).

■ Encourage the transfer of remittances by adopting sound macro-economic policies conducive to investment and growth and appropriate financial sector policy that encourages financial institutions and their outreach (AUF).

■ Create incentive strategies for remitters in commercial, entrepreneurial, savings and other productive activities (AUF).

Reducing Remittance Costs

■ By 2030, reduce to less than 3% the transaction costs of migrant remittances and eliminate remittance corridors with costs higher than 5% (SDG Target 10.C).

■ By 2030, reduce to less than 3% the transaction costs of migrant remittances and eliminate remittance corridors with costs higher than 5%. In addition, identify corridors for remittance transfers where the partners commit to substantially reducing the costs by 2020, from Europe to Africa and within Africa, in compliance with existing national legislation (VA).

■ Increase the volume of transfers through formal remittance channels (VA).

■ Develop mechanisms, services and effective financial products to facilitate the transfer of funds of emigrants and reduce the costs of these transfers (ACP).

■ In co-ordination with the African Institute for Remittances, determine ways to strengthen the infrastructure for remittance transfers that can be adopted and modified for implementation by individual states (MAP).

Optimizing Remittance Uses

■ Implement country-specific programmes, maximizing the impact of remittances notably in rural areas (VA).

■ Explore, identify and promote innovative financial instruments to channel remittances for development purposes (VA).

7. Incorporating Gendered Dimensions of Migration

Promoting Awareness

■ Promote equality of opportunity by strengthening gender-specific approaches to policies and activities concerning labour migration, particularly in recognition of the increasing feminization of labour migration (AUF).

■ Integrate a gender perspective in national and regional migration and management policies and strategies (AUF).

■ Promote campaigns to raise awareness about gender dimensions of migration among policy makers and personnel involved in managing migration (AUF).

■ Enhance collection, exchange and utilization of gender and age disaggregated data on migrants' economic activity, employment, skills, education, working conditions and social protection (JLMP).

Supporting Female Migrants

■ Eliminate all forms of violence against all women and girls in the public and private spheres, including trafficking and sexual and other types of exploitation (SDG Target 5.2).

■ Strengthen responses to the needs of migrant women, particularly ensuring that their health needs, labour rights and human rights are respected (AUF).

■ Take effective steps to counter migrant trafficking and smuggling and other illegal practices that specifically target and victimize migrant women (AUF).

■ Adopt measures to provide for the special needs of migrant women, children and youth (SADC EL).

8. Building Migrant Entrepreneurs

Entrepreneurial Support

■ Create new economic opportunities for young women and men through initiatives focused on, among others, targeted measures to create jobs and employment opportunities and stimulate entrepreneurship (VA).

■ Step up support to micro, small and medium-sized enterprises (SMEs) in the formal and informal sectors including through access to finance and micro-loans, training and incubation with particular focus on women, youth and rural populations (VA).

■ Promote migration schemes in small and medium-sized enterprises (SMEs) including training programmes for African entrepreneurs (VA).

■ Create incentive strategies for remitters in commercial, entrepreneurial, savings and other productive activities (AUF).

■ Mainstreaming and harmonization of status and rights of self-employed migrants (SA LMPF).

■ Support to self-employed migrant workers' organizations (SADC LMPF).

Cross-Border Trade

■ Support economic cross-border activities in border cities and markets (VA).

■ Mapping of main cross-border trade corridors and other activities adopted by self-employed migrants (SADC LMPF).

9. Engaging Diasporas

Building Linkages

■ Develop country-specific actions aiming at enhancing the development impact of migrant diasporas, both in the EU and associated countries and in Africa, to their country of origin. In this context, develop diaspora investment models aimed at leveraging migrants' savings for local business development and as a means of boosting local economic development (VA).

■ Further enhance the countries' outreach to and the knowledge of their diaspora (VA).

■ Encourage entities such as the EU/AC, AU, ILO and IOM to assist in fostering stronger relationships between African states and the African diaspora to create enabling conditions for the participation of migrants in the development of their home countries (AUF).

■ Make conscious efforts to reach out to diasporas and create channels of communication with them. Put appropriate institutional mechanisms in place that facilitate such communication and study the needs and incentives that might be required (AUF).

■ Create mechanisms for the strengthening of links between the countries of origin and African communities in the diaspora (ACP).

■ Develop a comprehensive set of policies and tools, including mapping exercises and outreach, related to diaspora engagement (MAP).

Encouraging Contributions

■ Encourage nationals abroad to contribute to the development of their state of origin through financial and human capital transfers such as short and long term return migration; and the transfer of knowledge and technology (AUF).

■ Promote the effective mobilization and utilization of diaspora funds for investment and development in the public and private sectors (AUF).

■ Establish a reliable database on the diaspora to determine its extent and magnitude and to promote networking and collaboration between experts in the state of origin and the diaspora (AUF).

■ Work towards the elaboration and implementation of policies that facilitate diaspora participation in the development of African countries (ACP).

■ Encourage inputs from the diaspora for the development of their countries of origin in the form of trade and investment activities, transfer of funds, competencies, technologies and by permanent or temporary participation in development projects (ACP).

10. Creating a Knowledge Platform

Migration Data Collection

■ By 2020, enhance capacity-building support to developing countries, including least developed countries and small island developing states, to increase significantly the availability of high quality, timely and reliable data that is disaggregated by income, gender, age, race, ethnicity, migratory status, disability, geographic location and other characteristics relevant in national contexts (SDG Target 17.18).

■ Enhance national and regional migration data collection, analysis and exchange to document the conditions and needs of migrant workers and their families (AUF).

■ Formulate and implement a common regional data standard and other initiatives to strengthen regional efforts to collect, analyze and share accurate basic information and data on the characteristics of migration in each country with a view to fostering migration and regional integration (AUF).

■ Enhance data collection, analysis and exchange on labour needs and supply in states of origin and destination in order to match labour skills with labour demand through comprehensive regional approaches (AUF).

■ Improve the quality of data on remittances and migration statistics to create a solid basis for policy action on remittances (AUF).

■ Establish a data bank on the scope of the brain drain phenomenon and qualified human resources (ACP).

■ Obtain relevant and comparable labour migration and labour market data (JLMP).

■ Develop standardized systems for data collection and analysis and harmonized migration indicators to be included in household surveys (MAP).

■ Make arrangements for better collection, management and sharing of data (SADC LMPF).

■ Standardize data collection mechanisms across member states from census and border control data sets (SADC LMPF).

■ Standardize migration modules within labour market surveys (SADC LMPF).

■ Mapping of industrial sectors reliant on migrant workers and understanding of the nature of reliance (SADC LMPF).

■ Mapping of socio-economic actors involved in the organization of low-skilled labour migration (labour brokers, recruitment agencies, ethnic networks and associations) (SADC LMPF).

Information Exchange

■ Ensure greater co-ordination between ministries and research institutions gathering migration data, including the establishment of a migration statistics unit responsible for co-ordinating the gathering of migration statistics (AUF).

■ Constitution of a regional forum for exchange of information, experience and perspective among governments, and through which a stocktaking of existing mechanisms and data could be undertaken, and bilateral and multilateral possibilities for data harmonization considered (AUF).

■ Establish appropriate mechanisms to bring together national focal points in charge of migration for regular information exchange (ACP).

■ Increase availability of data and statistics on migration (MAP).

■ Update the MIDSA Report on Migration Data Harmonization (published in 2007) for the purpose of identifying gaps in the collection, analysis, dissemination and harmonization of migration data (MAP).

■ Create a regular data collection mechanism and accessible platform within one existing member state statistics agency (SADC LMPF).

■ Promote labour migration data collection, analysis and exchange at regional and national levels (SADC Employment).

Research Priorities

■ Encourage research to generate information, identify problems and devise appropriate responses and strategies (AUF).

■ Explore the possibility of co-ordi nating studies and research on migration and development by existing institutions with a view to placing current and reliable information on migration at the disposal of states, sub-regional organizations and other users (ACP).

■ Initiate a SADC-wide migration profile study with a view to having a comprehensive overview of migration patterns and profiles within the SADC region and assessing the implications for policy development at the national and regional level (MAP).

■ Mapping of regional migration corridors of low-skilled workers (SADC LMPF).

Capacity-Building

■ Conduct training workshops on migration data collection, analysis and dissemination for participants from national statistical offices, national migration institutes and the SADC Statistical Department (MIDSA).

OPPORTUNITIES ASSESSMENT

- The SADC Secretariat has not been a leader to date in advancing a regional migration and development agenda, primarily because of capacity challenges and the responses of member states to past initiatives. EU support for the Secretariat may change this situation with several initiatives in planning or early stages of implementation. MIDSA offers a more flexible institutional structure but its ad hoc and non-binding nature means that an evaluation of its impact to date is a pre-condition for any support.

- Many of the recommended actions in the AU and SADC instruments have not yet been acted on and those that have tend to be targeted more at national governments than the region as a whole.

- The non-ratification of the key SADC migration-related protocols means that stakeholder engagement with a view to furthering ratification of protocols is unlikely to yield substantive results. The lukewarm reaction of member states to ratification of key instruments renders it unlikely that a donor-driven lobbying and implementation programme would achieve the desired effect. Donor funds are better spent on programming that would have as an outcome a clear demonstration to governments and regional bodies that migration does and can have beneficial migration and inclusive growth impacts for both countries of origin and destination.

- The Valetta Accord and AU Migration Framework and Common Position offer the SADC Secretariat an opportunity to take a lead role in designing and implementing programmes on migration for development and inclusive growth. In addition, the SADC Labour Migration Framework offers potential opportunities for optimizing the benefits of labour migration for employment purposes and, in particular, the target of each member state having a national labour migration policy by 2019. However,

the EU, ILO and the IOM are already fully engaged with the SADC Secretariat on the latter. The new round of EU funding for regional institution strengthening suggests that DFID regional programming might be better directed elsewhere.

- Harnessing migration for development and inclusive growth is not yet a priority for SADC member states. Regional programming would therefore more profitably be directed at projects and programmes of regional scope with the potential for a strong demonstration effect that at the same time bring tangible support and benefit to the target migrant groups and populations. The next section of the report develops this idea further by setting out a programming framework of potential actions for harnessing migration for development and inclusive growth and then using this framework to classify existing initiatives and identify areas of potential intervention.

- One possible alternative point of regional institutional engagement would be ongoing support for and strengthening of the MIDSA process. However, it is imperative to commission a comprehensive evaluation of the MIDSA process from its inception in order to assess its activities, achievements, outcomes and impacts with a view to determining whether it is a suitable vehicle for advancing a regional migration agenda on development and inclusive growth with tangible results. Potential points of intervention and leverage that could be facilitated and supported would need to be identified. A subsidiary point is that MIDSA is still largely reliant on donor funding and would, at the very least, require matching contributions from member states to ensure long-term self-reliance and sustainability.

- Some of the key areas for programming identified in the analysis have received limited attention, for example, skills migration, women's migration, remittance uses, diaspora engagement and migrant entrepreneurship.

- The challenge is to devise programmes that have a regional remit and impact and take account of the complexity of migration movements. The number of potential programming partners with regional capacity and focus is accordingly limited.

- While there is a growing research literature on migration and development, much of this is focused on South Africa and there is a dearth of regionally focused research programmes.

- Other regional programmes, such as the Freedom in Work programme in Asia, offer potential models but the issues and challenges in Southern Africa are somewhat different and would require reconfiguration for the specificities of this region.

STAKEHOLDER RECOMMENDATIONS

At the conclusion of the field interviews, the regional and national stakeholders were asked for their opinions on proposed directions and priorities for a new regional programme. NVIVO analysis showed a clear concern with three areas: (a) the existing governance mechanisms for migration management at the regional level and doubts about their capacity and effectiveness; (b) the absence or lack of a broad public and governmental awareness and recognition of the positive development impacts and implications of migration within, to and from Southern Africa; and (c) the large knowledge and information gaps that exist and how these might be addressed. We have used these three concerns to group, consolidate and classify specific recommendations.

TABLE 16: STAKEHOLDER PROGRAMMING RECOMMENDATIONS

Proposal	Comment
Migration Governance	
Interventions should focus on migration "push factors" in countries of origin including high rates of unemployment, poverty and inequality	Projects to address the perceived drivers of migration assume that migration is detrimental and have not been shown to be effective
FMM West Africa (the EU-ECOWAS programme) to support free movement of persons and migration in West Africa could serve as a model for Southern Africa	The new EU programme in support of SADC, COMESA and EAC is partially modelled on FMM West Africa
Support and technical assistance could be provided to the SADC Secretariat to facilitate ratification of the protocols and free movement	The new EU programme in support of SADC, COMESA and EAC is designed to provide such support
Support and technical assistance should be provided to member states to facilitate national labour migration plans and to integrate migration into national development planning	IOM and ILO are committed to implementing both of these suggestions
Support the implementation of the MIDSA process and identify areas to leverage for lobbying and advocacy	An evaluation of MIDSA's achievements and potential is needed to identify activities for support
Migration Capacity-Building	
Design and implement an in-service programme for capacity-building in migration management for development for government officials, as well as civil society and unions	Such a programme operated at the University of the Witwatersrand between 2006 and 2010. Evaluations were positive but the programme was expensive without matching funding from governments
Integrate migration and development into the curricula of all existing training programmes including home affairs and labour officials, police officers, nurses, social welfare staff, judiciary, prosecutors, and teachers as a means of making input on migration more accessible to those who would be dealing with migrants directly and on a daily basis	Prior to action on this suggestion, it would be necessary to compile a complete inventory of training courses (regional and national), to evaluate existing curricula and to design modules on harnessing migration for development
Design and implement a professional degree (MA) programme in Migration and Development to build the capacity and technical expertise of government, civil society, private sector and union planners and decision-makers, as well as building a regional pool of expertise	Discussions with Statistics South Africa suggest that they could be interested in such a programme
Migrant Working Conditions	
Improve the recruiting and working conditions of migrants, particularly women, in agriculture and domestic service	Some programmes are already targeting this issue though most are not regional but focus on one country. The idea of undertaking a pilot temporary work programme was mooted by TEBA. Further discussion would be necessary as the company has tried, without success, to extend the service it provides to mineworkers to the agricultural and domestic work sectors

Focus on the area of migrant protection. This could include work at institutional level; for example, strengthening the national referral mechanism for victims of trafficking, unaccompanied migrant children and vulnerable migrants, training on migrant protection, working with multi-sectoral groups at border posts across the region, such as border guards and social services. Such training could include screening for vulnerabilities, proper referral, provision of protection, and voluntary return and reintegration strategies	This suggestion needs to be considered seriously either as an objective in itself (along the lines of previous IOM programming) or as one element of a more targeted programme, e.g. focused on domestic workers or farmworkers
Continue work on remittances. Conduct a study on the usage and impact of remittances and use the study to develop a community development programme so that remittances are not used only for basic needs but also for setting up businesses and investment	FinMark Trust has worked on remittances flows and reducing remittance costs. The next logical step is to design and support innovative programmes that encourage the productive use of investments
Develop a framework and roadmap for small-scale traders	This proposal was the only one to target the informal economy explicitly. Although there was no indication what the roadmap would achieve, it could be the first step in a larger programme of support for informal entrepreneurship
Facilitate engagement with the diaspora	No additional suggestions were provided but diaspora engagement is a central pillar of the instruments reviewed and migration and development programming more generally
Migration Data Collection and Use	
Help to generate the evidence that would dispel myths about migration and demonstrate that it has positive development outcomes for countries of origin and destination and migrants themselves	There are major gaps in our understanding of migration at the regional level and a great deal of misinformation that leads to negative and xenophobic outcomes. Most research to date has focused on proving the existence of rights abuse, understanding its causes and documenting the hardships experienced by migrants. There is much less evidence on migrants as active agents, seeking to better their lives and generating positive impacts for development and inclusive growth
Support the collection, analysis and use of migration data across the region as an aid to policy-making. This could be a combination of collecting and collating existing data and generating new data through modules in labour force surveys and dedicated household migration surveys	Some respondents thought it would be useful to have a central facility for the collection, organization and dissemination of migration data at the regional level; others were sceptical. Some were hesitant about having a central facility for the collection, organization and dissemination of migration data at the regional level but thought it could work if there were clear agreements on who would use it. It was mentioned that it could have potential if it was independently run but it would not be sustainable if donor funding runs out. Data collection and management is already a central pillar of the new EU regional support programme though the details have yet to be worked out

GENDER AND MIGRATION PROGRAMMING FOR DEVELOPMENT AND INCLUSIVE GROWTH

The Programming Framework can be used by stakeholders as a tool to identify potential development-related migration programmes and interventions. We reviewed existing programming in Southern Africa and identified themes and areas that are relatively neglected or underdeveloped and could constitute central entry points for programming. The PF is reproduced below with the recommended action areas highlighted.

Our main recommendation is for a programme on Gender and Migration for Development and Inclusive Growth in Southern Africa. Our general starting point is the July 2016 ODI Briefing Paper "Women on the Move: Migration, Gender Equality and the 2030 Agenda for Sustainable Development" and the UN-INSTRAW/UNDP Report on "Gender,

TABLE 17: PROPOSED ENTRY POINTS IN PROGRAMMING FRAMEWORK

Issue	Entry Points
Ensuring Rights and Protections for Migrants	Eliminating Exploitation
Adding Value to Remittances	Optimizing Remittance Uses
Incorporating Gender Dimensions of Migration	Supporting Female Migrants
Building Migrant Entrepreneurs	Entrepreneurial Support
Engaging Diasporas	Encouraging Contributions
Creating a Knowledge Platform	Research Priorities

Migration and Gender-Responsive Local Development".[81] As the latter notes:

> *Studying the phenomena of migration and remittances from a gender perspective…has yielded an understanding of the differences between women's and men's migratory experiences, the ways in which gender relations are influenced or reinforced, and which factors promote greater gender equity. In order for women's participation in the migratory process to contribute to development, both in origin and destination countries, it is necessary to go beyond isolated micro-projects in order to enact public policies that eliminate obstacles to their autonomy. The rise in women's independent migration can increase their decision-making power, but certain factors must be taken into account in order to guarantee equitable development including: the division of reproductive labour, access to education and equal pay, access to land and credit and the guarantee of their rights of association and labour, among others.[82]*

Entry Point One: Building a Gendered Knowledge Base

One of the recurrent themes in the stakeholder interviews was (a) the limited public availability and utility of official data on migration; and (b) the lack of knowledge about migration causes, volumes, experiences and impacts. The information that does exist comes from "add-on" questions to national or sample surveys designed for other purposes and small-scale, local case studies on migration whose findings are not necessarily representative of the wider population of migrants. A common failing of official data and the case-study research literature is the absence of systematic and generalizable information on the gendered nature of migration. In order to provide detailed, policy-relevant, gender-disaggregated data on migration and its development impacts, a different methodological approach is needed. Our recommendation is for the collection of national migration data at the household level in countries of origin and destination through the implementation of nationally representative surveys of migrant-sending households.

The knowledge and policy value of this kind of methodology is clearly illustrated by previous projects whose findings are widely cited as the only authoritative sources of data on all aspects of migration in the SADC region, including its gender dimensions. Survey instruments and sampling strategies should be designed and implemented in such a way as to permit not merely comparison between male and female

migrants, but knowledge and understanding of various household forms and intra-household gender relations and dynamics as they affect and are affected by migration. These surveys would ensure the collection of gender-disaggregated data on a range of critical migration and development issues including migration drivers, migrant characteristics and motivations, migrant occupations and remitting behaviour, remittance channels and uses, and general migration impacts at the household, community and national scales.

Only two countries in the SADC have conducted National Migration Surveys in the past: Botswana in 1980 and Namibia in 1998. Both surveys provided detailed insights into the dimensions and drivers of internal and international migration in these countries at the time but are now extremely dated. The World Bank and African Development Bank Africa Migration Project conducted Migration and Remittances Household Surveys in Burkina Faso, Kenya, Nigeria, Senegal, South Africa, and Uganda in 2009-2010. The surveys used a standardized methodology developed by the World Bank and were conducted by primarily country-based researchers and institutions during 2009 and 2010. They covered recent migration and remittance trends, housing conditions, household assets and expenditures, use of financial services, internal and international migration and remittances from former and non-former household members. Collectively, say the Banks, "these surveys provide unique data and a new research methodology for collecting information on migration and remittances in Sub-Saharan Africa."[83]

The Southern African Migration Programme (SAMP) conducted two nationally representative household surveys in six countries in the SADC (Botswana, Lesotho, Mozambique, Namibia, Swaziland and Zimbabwe) in 2005 and 2006. The first (the Migration and Remittances Survey or MARS) focused on migrant-sending households, while the second (the Migration and Poverty Survey or MAPS) sampled migrant and non-migrant households. The surveys covered a wide range of household and individual migrant characteristics, migration motives and behaviours, migrant occupations and remitting practices, and the relationship between migration and local development as well as migration and gender.[84] These surveys have and continue to be widely cited but represent the situation a decade ago. They do not capture, for example, recent evidence that some migration streams are becoming more permanent in nature.

We recommend another round of national migration surveys using these tested methodologies and instruments in as many SADC countries as funding allows. There is an urgent need for the kind of current and comprehensive data and information that such surveys provide. As well as providing the critical gender-disaggregated information on migration and development that does not currently exist, the findings could be used to build the evidence-based demonstration effect of the possibilities for further harnessing migration for development and inclusive growth. The data would also inform the development and implementation of the other work packages suggested below. Potential outcomes include the following:

- Filling of information and data gaps on the relationships between migration, development and inclusive growth;

- Current, actionable information on migration dynamics and development impacts and potential in countries of origin and destination, including differentiation by gender and household type;

- Demonstration effect of positive development implications of migration by men and women in the region, to support regional co-operation and management initiatives including ratification of protocols and other regional initiatives such as MIDSA; and

- Design of gender-based programmes and interventions based on solid and reliable information on gender dimensions of migration.

Entry Point Two: Protecting Female Migrants in Domestic Work

The SADC Labour Migration Framework has as two of its objectives (a) strengthening protection of the rights of migrant workers; and (b) harnessing positive gender considerations and demographic dividends. These objectives urgently need to be realized in the low-wage sectors in which migrant women and girls tend to concentrate, especially domestic work. The Preamble to the 2011 Domestic Workers Convention notes that "domestic work continues to be undervalued and invisible and is mainly carried out by women and girls, many of whom are migrants or members of disadvantaged communities and who are particularly vulnerable to discrimination in respect of conditions of employment and of work, and to other abuses of human rights."[85] A programme focus on the rights and protection of women and girl migrants would materially advance these objectives and potentially enhance implementation of the Labour Migration Framework and the Domestic Workers Convention.

The field research confirmed that several civil society groups, NGOs, unions and international organizations are beginning to focus their attention on the precarious employment of migrant women. We therefore recommend a regional programme directed at improving the conditions for women and youth migrating to and working in the domestic service sector. Existing research tends to be of a narrow case-study nature but has identified some of the major challenges faced by women migrants recruited by labour brokers and others, travelling to places of employment, poor treatment by employers and constant vulnerability to exploitation and deportation due to uncertain legal status. The obligations enshrined in the Domestic Workers Convention contain commitments to domestic workers for the effective promotion and protection of human rights including the right to freedom of association and collective bargaining; the elimination of all forms of forced or compulsory labour; the effective abolition of child labour; and the elimination of discrimination in respect of employment and occupation. The Convention also promotes the need for a minimum wage; the right to a safe and healthy work environment; effective protection against all forms of abuse, harassment and violence; enjoyment of fair terms of employment as well as decent working and living conditions; the use by employers of appropriate, verifiable and easily understandable written contracts; social security protection and effective access to courts, tribunals and other dispute resolution mechanisms.

The precarious legal position of migrant domestic workers makes it easier for employers to circumvent some or all of these commitments. The Convention also elucidates several goals that apply specifically to migrants including that:

- Migrant domestic workers who are recruited in one country for domestic work in another receive a written job offer, or contract of employment that is enforceable in the country in which the work is to be performed, prior to crossing national borders for the purpose of taking up the domestic work to which the offer or contract applies; and

- To effectively protect domestic workers, including migrant domestic workers recruited or placed by private employment agencies, against abusive practices, it is necessary to (a) determine the conditions governing the operation of private employment agencies recruiting or placing domestic workers; (b) ensure that adequate machinery and procedures exist for the investigation of complaints, alleged abuses and fraudulent practices concerning the activities of private employment agencies in relation to domestic workers; (c) adopt all necessary and appropriate measures to provide adequate protection for and prevent abuses of domestic workers recruited or placed in its territory by private employment agencies; (d) recruiting of domestic workers in one country for work in another should ideally be governed by bilateral, regional or multilateral agreements to prevent abuses and fraudulent practices in recruitment, placement and employment; and (e) take measures to ensure that fees charged by private employment agencies are not deducted from the remuneration of domestic workers.

The extent to which employers, labour brokers and governments are in breach of the Convention is unknown and needs to be systematically researched. The largely informal, unorganized nature of domestic worker recruitment in this region makes it difficult to assess or monitor, but this only adds to the urgency of doing so. Further, programmes to inform and educate domestic workers of their rights, and employers and employment agencies of their obligations, are needed.

Because most migrant women in domestic work tend to move along major migration corridors, there is a strong case for adopting a corridor-focused approach to programme implementation. Two corridors, in particular, are known to be significant avenues for migrant women in domestic work: the Zimbabwe-Gauteng-Western Cape corridor and the Lesotho-Gauteng corridor. By focusing attention on these two corridors, identifying the challenges and obstacles facing migrant domestic workers and materially affecting the employment conditions of migrant women, this work package can have a strong demonstration effect on the need to protect and guarantee the rights of vulnerable workers and ensure that they benefit from, and contribute to, inclusive economic growth.

The Work in Freedom programme in Asia is a potential model for integrated programming on migrant domestic worker protection in Southern Africa and therefore requires additional comment. Its primary aim is to combat trafficking in women and girls from South-East Asia to the garment and domestic work sectors in major destination countries including Jordan, Lebanon and the United Arab Emirates. While trafficking is a concern in Southern Africa generally, there is less evidence that it is a significant problem in relation to employment in domestic service. The Work in Freedom programme has a main focus on promoting ethical and good industry practices among the intermediaries between countries of origin and destination in the so-called "recruitment industry."

The primary differences between the Work in Freedom corridors and those in Southern Africa are (a) the length and complexity of navigating the corridors. In Southern Africa, geographical proximity and ease of overland travel by minibus taxi means that informal, individualized migration is much more feasible; (b) the reliance of Asian migrants on unscrupulous intermediaries given the cost and logistical challenges of long-distance migration. While there is some

evidence of the involvement of formal and informal labour brokers in recruiting and placing farm and domestic workers, more research is needed on how the system works and if and how the basic rights of migrants are violated; (c) while migrants in the Work in Freedom corridors are generally working legally in the destination country, this is not often the case in Southern Africa. Because irregular migration and work status make migrants vulnerable to a set of abuses in the workplace and in the neighbourhoods in which they live, this would need to be a central focus in a programme for Southern Africa.

Potential outcomes of programming in this area include the following:

- Implementation and monitoring of the protections enshrined in the Domestic Workers Convention in countries that have ratified the Convention;

- Identification of practices that are in breach of the Convention in non-ratifying countries;

- New and better evidence generated on women and girl migrants in low-wage employment and the nature, drivers and impacts of precarious employment in domestic work;

- Women and girls enjoy greater protection while migrating and in the workplace in low-wage sectors;

- Maximizing economic and other benefits to households and communities from the migration of women and girls into low-wage sectors in other countries;

- Private sector recruitment agencies and labour brokers adopt ethical principles and practices, in line with fair recruitment standards; and

- New legal or policy initiatives are implemented to protect and guarantee the rights of women migrant workers (in transit and in the workplace).

Entry Point Three: Maximizing Remittance Impacts for Women Migrants

Several programmes have been designed to understand remitting practices and channels, improve financial literacy and reduce the costs of remitting, especially by SAMP (2005-2008)[86] and FinMark Trust.[87] With the exception of one major but dated study by SAMP, little attention has been paid to the gender dimensions of remitting in Southern Africa.[88] The SAMP study suggested that:

- For most migrant-sending households, migrant remittances form the main source of household income. The proportion of male and female migrants sending remittances varied from country to country but was over two-thirds of all female migrants in each country;

- The amounts of money remitted by female migrants were significantly lower than those of male migrants, in part reflecting women migrants' lower levels of income and employment security. However, women remit a greater proportion of their earnings;

- Lesotho's female migrants remitted larger sums than female migrants from any of the other countries;

- Many female migrants come from female-centred households, with no husband or male partner. Women's remittances are especially significant to such households as the primary – often only – source of household income;

- The main uses of remittances from both male and female migrant-sending households were expenditures on the basic commodities of food, domestic fuel and clothing, and fundamental services such as schooling, health care and transport;

- There were important gender differences, as well as differences between countries, in the amounts of monthly expenditure on particular categories of expenses; and

- As the primary source of income for the majority of households, remittance earnings are vital in enabling households to meet their basic needs. Food is the most common annual expenditure of remittance money in both male and female migrant-sending households. Second in all countries is either clothing or school fees. Remittances do not appear to be spent on non-essential or luxury items, but nor are they commonly directed towards savings or investment in business or other productive activities.

While there is a need for updated regional data on the gendered dimensions of remitting (which could be garnered through Work Package One), the priority is to devise practical, actionable programmes of support which would turn remittances from meeting basic household consumption needs into sources of productive investment by recipients at the household and community levels. There are anecdotal examples of this: for example, Lesotho's spaza shops and taxi-cab industries were largely financed in the start-up phase by migrant remittances. However, this work package should seek to understand, perhaps through pilot studies, (a) the kinds of self-help organizations established by women

(including *stokvels*, savings clubs, burial societies, egg circles and co-operatives) and the ways in which individual and collective remitting might enhance their activities; (b) how financial remittances might enhance and meet women's micro-entrepreneurship needs for start-up and working capital, perhaps through financial matching programmes; and (c) whether there is evidence of social remittances, such as changed perceptions of gender roles, affecting women's economic and entrepreneurial activity in migrant-sending communities.

There is considerable global and regional debate about how best to harness remittances for development and inclusive growth.[89] The available evidence suggests that remittances build three forms of capital: (a) human capital through expenditures on food purchase, education, clothing, shelter, transportation and medical expenses. This shows the importance of remittances to the well-being of the household and especially its younger members (through improved food security, education and health); (b) physical capital through savings and investment in, for example, agricultural inputs such as seed, fertilizer and tractor hire; and (c) financial capital through micro-enterprise start-ups and expansion. The impacts of remitting on physical and financial capital remain largely in the realm of assertion rather than demonstration.

IFAD's Scaling Up Remittances (SURE) programme is a potential model for this programme. As IFAD notes, "the impact of remittances is dramatically enhanced when linked to other financial services such as savings, insurance and loan products. Inclusive financial systems and innovative partnerships between financial institutions and remittance operators can produce significant benefits by easing competition and reducing costs, thereby offering more resources to the poor and increased options for families to use their capital to its maximum potential. In addition, migrants' capital savings have been proven successful at promoting entrepreneurship and local economic development back home."[90] IFAD's rural focus assumes, as does much of the literature, that such programmes should be rural-focused whereas it is actually more likely that opportunities for the productive use of remittances are greater in urban areas. Thus, we suggest that programming should focus more on urban-urban remitting to have tangible results and benefits for inclusive growth. Potential outcomes include:

- Improved knowledge base on the uses of individual and collective remittances by recipient households and communities including support for productive use of remittances to establish and grow micro-enterprises (especially by women and youth), the extent and potential of collective remitting as a source of start-up capital and obstacles and challenges faced by actual and potential micro-entrepreneurs;

- Identification of obstacles, challenges and opportunities for leveraging remittances to foster micro-enterprise start-ups and development;

- Demonstration effect of support of innovative, best-practice solutions for productive use of remittances; and

- Micro-enterprises developed and job creation enhanced, especially by women entrepreneurs, as part of the programme to harness remittances for development and inclusive growth.

Entry Point Four: Enhancing Female Migrant Entrepreneurship

In cities throughout South Africa, migrants from other countries (including forced migrants) are involved in the establishment of small businesses to support themselves and their families and to generate remittances to send back to their home countries. As many as 60% of migrant small business owners in South Africa are remitters. There is a common (mis)perception that migrant entrepreneurs are "survivalists," forced to establish their businesses because of a failure to obtain formal employment and operating with razor thin margins. However, there is a growing body of research that highlights the entrepreneurial orientation and motivation of the majority of migrant business owners. Their innovative business strategies have also been highlighted, as have the challenges they face in establishing, operating and growing their businesses. Studies have identified the following as major business challenges: (a) economic challenges including shortages of start-up capital, lack of access to credit, competition from formal sector outlets and suppliers over-charging; (b) social challenges such as prejudice against their nationality and xenophobic attacks; and (c) security challenges such as crime and theft, confiscation of goods by the police, harassment and demands for bribes and protection money, and physical attacks by the police. Most migrant entrepreneurs start their businesses with personal savings as they are unable to access bank loans and other sources of start-up capital.

Despite these problems, migrant entrepreneurs deliver important development benefits to countries of origin (through remittances) and destination (including cheaper foodstuffs and consumables, credit facilities, and job creation, as well as generating economic profits for formal sector suppliers such as wholesalers and supermarkets). One aspect of migrant entrepreneurship in which women are particularly involved is running businesses in their own countries and using cross-border trading as a strategy to build their businesses, profits and impacts. Migrant entrepreneurs are still in need of various programmes of support to address some of the challenges they face and to maximize their entrepreneurial activities and contributions. There is a dearth of programmes supporting migrant women's small and micro-entrepreneurship activities and initiatives in Southern Africa. Migrants are generally excluded from government training and support programmes.

There are several models that could be used and adapted to the specific circumstances of actual and aspirant migrant women entrepreneurs in SADC. These include the US African Women's Entrepreneurship Program, which is described as an outreach, education and engagement initiative that targets African women entrepreneurs to promote business growth, increase trade, create better business environments, and empower African women entrepreneurs to become voices of change in their communities.[91] Another example is the ILO's Women's Entrepreneurship Development Programme, which "works with service providers promoting entrepreneurship development (financial, non-financial, public, private, associative, freelance) and builds their capacity to better support women entrepreneurs to start and grow their businesses. It also works towards creating a more positive enabling environment for WED, by supporting assessments of the situation, and working with governments and policy makers to remove the specific gender barriers that women entrepreneurs may face."[92] This programme has primarily focused on East Africa but a similar programme in Southern Africa would be of considerable benefit. Potential outcomes of programming are as follows:

- New knowledge for public education and policy-making on the contributions of male and female migrant entrepreneurs to the development of host and home countries;

- Improved regulatory and operating environment for migrant entrepreneurship;

- Ability of migrant entrepreneurs to run businesses more effectively and profitably, create jobs and enter partnerships with local entrepreneurs;

- Empowering of women migrant entrepreneurs to establish and grow their in-country and cross-border businesses; and

- Development of best-practice solutions to assist growth of migrant-owned SMEs across the region.

Entry Point Five: Deploying Diaspora Skills for Women/Youth Empowerment

There is growing interest in the actual and potential role of diasporas as a resource for development and inclusive growth in Africa. Chikezie argues that diasporas possess five forms of diaspora capital (the "5 Cs"): intellectual capital, financial capital, political capital, cultural capital and social capital.[93] In order for African governments and regional organizations to engage effectively with diasporas, it is important to understand what motivates diasporas to be involved in African development: the "3 Ps" of pecuniary interests, private interests and public philanthropic interests.[94] As noted above, the Southern African region has a significant global diaspora. Most diaspora engagement programmes and projects have

been developed by national governments (though Southern African governments are not generally among them). However, "in reinforcing the African diaspora's contribution to development, there remains a critical role for regional bodies…and even regional economic institutions."[95]

The global Southern African diaspora represents a large skills and expertise pool, several million strong, that has not yet been effectively leveraged for development by Southern African countries. Some countries, such as Zambia and Zimbabwe, have official diaspora engagement policies. Others are being developed (Table 18). South Africa has declared its intention to engage with the diaspora in the new Green Paper. The Zambian government has been the most proactive, establishing a Diaspora Liaison Office at Presidential level. Most recently, in September 2015,

TABLE 18: DIASPORA ENGAGEMENT POLICIES OF SADC GOVERNMENTS

Country/ Region	Policy Initiatives and Institutions	Priorities
AU	Citizens and Diaspora Directorate http://www.african-union.africa-newsroom.com/press/citizens-and-diaspora-directorate-cido-towards-creating-a-diaspora-engagement-toolkit?lang=en	Facilitate diaspora engagement activities and policies Diaspora engagement toolkit
Angola	Institute of the Angolan Communities Abroad and Consulate Affairs	Business investment consular workshops
Botswana	No formal policies	
DRC[96]	No formal policies	
Lesotho[97]	No formal policies	
Mauritius	Mauritius Diaspora Scheme http://www.diaspora.mu/government.aspx	Return migration
Madagascar	2015 Diaspora Directorate http://www.diplomatie.gov.mg/index.php?categorie10/diaspora-malagasy	Strengthening linkages, socio-economic projects, promoting youth
Malawi	2012 Diaspora Engagement Programme and Diaspora Affairs Unit in Ministry Co-operation http://www.foreignaffairs.gov.mw/index.php/diaspora-services/overview	Remittances, investments, skills transfer
Mozambique	2014 Strategy for Diaspora Engagement in National Development https://www.iom.int/news/mozambique-launches-diaspora-engagement-strategy National Institute for Mozambican Communities in the Diaspora (INACE) IOM Diaspora Engagement Project https://developmentfund.iom.int/news/iom-mozambique-launch-diaspora-engagement-project	Develop national diaspora engagement policy
Namibia	Diaspora policy in development https://www.nbc.na/news/namibia-develop-migration-policy-namibians-diaspora.1004	
South Africa[98]	Hosted 2012 Global African Diaspora Summit http://www.dirco.gov.za/diaspora/index.html Diaspora engagement policy proposed in 2016 Green Paper on International Migration	
Swaziland	No formal policies	
Tanzania[99]	Diaspora Engagement and Opportunity Department in Ministry of Foreign Affairs and International Development (MFAIC) http://www.foreign.go.tz/index.php/en/about/diaspora-engagement-and-opportunities-division Tanzania Diaspora Conference 2016 http://tzdiaspora.org/concept-notes.html Zanzibar Diaspora http://www.zanzibardiaspora.go.tz/	Investment, tourism, diaspora database
Zambia	Diaspora Liaison Office in President's Office National policy framework in development[100]	Wide-ranging framework of activities
Zimbabwe	2016 National Diaspora Policy http://www.zimbabwesituation.com/news/zimsit-m-cabinet-approves-national-diaspora-policy/ Zimbabwe National Diaspora Directorate https://www.iom.int/news/zimbabwe-launches-national-diaspora-directorate	Skills transfer, productive use of remittances

the Zambian diaspora association in the UK (DfAD) organized a conference in London on Southern African Diaspora Communities in the UK. DfAD made two main points of relevance: first, that policies should facilitate the setup of sound and informed regulatory frameworks for the diaspora to invest in development and job creation; and second, that the policy should ensure the portability of skills and benefits that would recognize the diaspora's professional and vocational qualifications. By identifying the existence of a *Southern* African diaspora, the event went beyond the usual conceptualization of individual countries engaging with their own national diasporas abroad. This is where there is a major programming gap to be filled, i.e. recognition of and engagement with the regional diaspora at a regional level.

The general literature on diaspora engagement has identified a range of potential areas including remittances, investment, philanthropy, tourism, skills and knowledge transfer and some countries, such as the Philippines, have instituted a range of extremely successful diaspora engagement policies. A regional diaspora engagement policy for Southern Africa as a whole needs to be based on (a) a mapping of existing development-related initiatives by members of diasporas within and from Southern Africa; (b) information about the types of engagement activities that members of the diaspora are interested in supporting or participating in at the regional level; for example, Zimbabweans or South Africans abroad being willing to engage in skills transfer anywhere in the SADC region; and (c) the establishment of mechanisms that would enable and facilitate engagement at the regional level, perhaps initially in the form of a platform or marketplace for being part of or supporting regional projects. To align this proposal with the general theme of gender and migration, such a programme could have a focus on developing diaspora support for projects and programmes that specifically target enhancing gender equity and women's empowerment. Highlighting the achievements and tapping the skills of successful women in the diaspora could be a potential means of changing gender perceptions and empowering women in the region.

Potential outcomes include:

- Improved knowledge base on current forms of regional engagement by the Southern African diaspora, including the role and significance of gender;

- Creation of a platform or marketplace for the exchange of ideas and information about engagement possibilities at the regional level;

- Utilization by civil society actors and the private sector of the skills of men and women in the diaspora in development-oriented activities and programmes;

- Demonstration effect of successful skills and knowledge transfer programme with impact at the regional level; and

- Commitment by members of the diaspora from individual countries to a regional vision of diaspora engagement.

APPENDIX A: STAKEHOLDER CONSULTATIONS

Fieldwork was undertaken by a team of four fieldworkers from Southern Hemisphere Consulting. Country visits were undertaken to South Africa, Mozambique, Botswana and Zimbabwe. Interviews were conducted face to face in-country, where possible, or telephonically. A total of 60 interviews with 86 interviewees were done.

Regional-level interviews		
Stakeholder group	**Ministry/organization**	**Detail**
DFID regional office	DFID	Fiona Clark and Joel Harding
Donors and international agencies implementing programmes with a regional focus	USAID USAID Democracy and Governance Regional General Development Office	Laura Berger, democracy HR and governance team leader Paula van Dyk, democracy HR and governance senior programme specialist
	Swiss Agency for Development and Co-operation	Juliane Ineichen, deputy regional director of co-operation
	Save the Children (Southern and Eastern Africa)	Melinda van Zyl, Eastern and Southern Africa senior manager for child migration
Regional organizations (intergovernmental and non-governmental)	International Alliance of Street Vendor Organizations	Pat Horn
	SADC Cross-Border Traders Association	Francis Ngambi
	OSISA	Alice Kanengoni
	Southern African Trust	Christabel Phiri
	Finmark Trust	Brendan Pearce, head of programmes
Multilaterals	IOM Regional/MIDSA	Richard Ots and Jo Rispoli
	UNHCR	Amanuel Tesfayesus Mehari
	UNDP	Osten Chulu
	ILO	Joni Musabayana, Deputy Director: ILO
Regional organizations	African Union	Peter Mudungwe, Migration Advisor for African Union commission
	EU	Mary Horvers, EU attaché , Regional Co-operation
	GIZ	Phillip Madelung, programme manager, Co-operation for the Enhancement of SADC Regional Economic Integration (CESARE)

Country-level interviews for South Africa		
Stakeholder group	**Ministry/organization**	**Detail**
Affected groups	Scalabrini Centre	Miranda Madikane, Director
	Lawyers for Human Rights (LHR)	Jacob van Garderen and David Cote
Donors and international agencies implementing programmes with a national focus	IOM South Africa	Josiah Ogina
	EU Delegation to South Africa	Belen Calvo, political counsellor
National government representatives (e.g. immigration, social welfare, labour)	Statistics South Africa	Miranda Mafafo and Themba Mohoto
	Department of Health	Barry Kistnasamy, Compensation Commissioner for Occupational Diseases
	Department of Home Affairs	Lionel Isaacs
	Department of Labour	Esther Tloane and three colleagues
Academic institutions	GCRO	Sally Peberdy
	African Centre for Migration & Society: University of the Witwatersrand	Ingrid Palmary
		Loren Landau
Union	COSATU	Bongani Masuku, Secretary, International Department

Country-level interviews for Botswana		
Stakeholder group	**Ministry/organization**	**Detail**
Donors	GIZ	Sophia Gallina and Adane Ghebremeskel
	Frederick-Ebert Stiftung	Ulrich Golaszinski
	USAID Southern Africa Trade Hub	Gregory Maassen and Brian McCotter
Multilaterals	UNHCR	Mandipa Machacha
	IOM Botswana	Sikhulile Dhlamini
Unions	Botswana Federation of Trade Unions	Gadzani Mhotsha
Academic institutions	University of Botswana	Teresa Galvin
	University of Botswana	David Mandiyanike

Country-level interviews for Mozambique		
Stakeholder group	**Ministry/organization**	**Detail**
Donors and international agencies implementing programmes with a national focus	IOM	Jason Theede, Programme Manager: Labour Migration and Development / Migration and Health Ruth Krcmar, Programme Coordinator: Migrant Assistance / Integrated Border Management
	GIZ	Peter Pfaumann, Country Director
	UN Women	Ondina da Barca Vieira, Gender Programme Specialist
Affected groups	Mukhero Cross-Border Traders' Association	Novela Sudecar, Director
Unions	Mozambique Workers' Organization (OTM)	Florencio Quetane, Head of Chamber General Secretary Antonio Paunde Machuquela, Head of Office of Communication, Image and International Relations
Academic institutions	Eduardo Mondlane University, Faculty of Arts and Social Sciences, Centre for Policy Analysis	Ines Macamo Raimondo, Deputy Dean of Faculty of Arts and Social Sciences Ramos Cardoso Muanamoha, Chief of Department

Country-level interviews for Zimbabwe		
Stakeholder group	**Ministry/organization**	**Detail**
Donor	DFID country office (Zimbabwe)	Jessica Pettiprez, Social Development Advisor
Affected groups	Cross-Border Traders' Association	Augustine Tawanda, Secretary General Abel Jaridi, Treasurer
	Labour and Economic Development Research Institute Zimbabwe (LEDRIZ)	Nyasha Muchinchwa, Researcher
Multilaterals	ILO – Zimbabwe and Namibia office	Adolphus Chinomwe, Senior Programme Officer Hopolang Phororo, Director
	IOM	Lily Sanya, head of mission Knowledge Mareyanadzo, government liaison
	UN Women	Rumbidzai Dube, Senior GBV co-ordinator
	UNICEF	Allet Sibanda, programme officer CP Noriko Izumi, Chief CP Catherine Makoni, Gender and HR Specialist
Government	Ministry of Labour	Langton Ngorima, Acting Deputy Director M.V. Hanga, Principal Labour Officer M Parakokwa, Principal Labour Officer T.C. Jongwe, Principal Labour Officer S.T. Kadzima, Principal Labour Officer
Private sector	Zimbabwe National Chamber of Commerce	C. Mugaga, CEO
Unions	Zimbabwe Council of Trade Unions	Michael Kandukutu, national organizer Fiona Magaya, gender co-ordinator
Academic institution	University of Zimbabwe	Innocent Chirisa

APPENDIX B: LIST OF KEY SOURCES

African Development Bank, *African Development Report 2014: Regional Integration for Inclusive Growth* (Abidjan, 2014).

S. Angenendt, *Triple-Win Migration: Challenges and Opportunities*. Migration Strategy Group, German Marshall Fund of US, 2014.

R. Amit, "Paying for Protection: Corruption in South Africa's Asylum System" *Migration Information Source*, 5 November 2015.

M. Apleni, "An Overview of the New Immigration Laws and Regulations and their Implications" Presentation to Parliamentary Portfolio Committee on Home Affairs, 23 April 2015.

D. Budlender, "Decent Work for Domestic Workers" Study for Services Sector Education and Training Sector, CASE, Johannesburg, 2010.

D. Budlender, *Improving the Quality of Available Statistics on Foreign Labour in South Africa: Existing Data Sets*. MiWORC Report No. 2, Johannesburg, 2013.

C. Chikezie, "Reinforcing the Contributions of African Diasporas to Development" In S. Plaza and D. Ratha, (eds.), *Diaspora for Development in Africa* (Washington DC, 2011), pp. 261-82.

J. Crush, "Towards the Triple Win: Lower-Skilled Labour Migration to South Africa", Paper for Colloquium on a New International Migration Policy Paradigm for South Africa, Department of Home Affairs, 2015.

J. Crush and M. Caesar, *Food Remittances: Migration and Food Security in Africa*. SAMP Migration Policy Series No. 72, Cape Town, 2016.

J. Crush, A. Chikanda and C. Skinner, (eds.), *Mean Streets: Migration, Xenophobia and Informality in South Africa* (Ottawa and Cape Town, 2015).

J. Crush and D. Tevera (eds.), *Zimbabwe's Exodus: Crisis, Migration, Survival* (Cape Town, 2010).

J. Crush and W. Pendleton, "Remitting for Survival: Rethinking the Development Potential of Remittances in Southern Africa" *Global Development Studies* 5(3/4) (2009): 53-84.

J. Crush, V. Williams and P. Nicholson, "Migrants' Rights After Apartheid: South African Responses to the ICRMW" In P. de Guchteneire et al, *Migration and Human Rights: The United Nations Convention on Migrant Workers' Rights* (Cambridge and Paris, 2009), pp. 247-77.

B. Deacon, M. Olivier and R. Beremauro, *Social Security and Social Protection of Migrants in South Africa and SADC*. MiWorc Report No. 8, Johannesburg, 2013.

Department of Home Affairs, "2015 Asylum Statistics: Analysis and Trends for the Period January to December" Portfolio Committee on Home Affairs, 23 April 2015.

Department of Home Affairs, *Green Paper on International Migration in South Africa* (Pretoria, 2016), p. 30.

N. Dinat and S. Peberdy, *Migrants in Domestic Work in South Africa*. SAMP Migration Policy Series No. 40, Johannesburg, 2005.

B. Dodson, "Gender, Migration and Livelihoods: Migrant Women in Southern Africa" In N. Piper (ed.), *New Perspectives on Gender and Migration* (London, 2013).

B. Dodson and J. Crush, *Migration Governance and Migrant Rights in the Southern African Development Community (SADC)*. UNRISD Research Paper 2015-3, Geneva, 2015.

B. Dodson et al, *Gender, Migration and Remittances in Southern Africa*. SAMP Migration Policy Series No. 49, Cape Town, 2008.

DNA Economics, *The South Africa-SADC Remittance Channel*. Report for FinMark Trust, February 2012.

R. Ehrlich, "A Century of Miners' Compensation in South Africa" *American Journal of Industrial Medicine* 55(2012).

C. Fauvelle-Aymar, *Migration and Employment in South Africa: An Econometric Analysis of Domestic and International Migrants*. MiWorc Report No. 6, ACMS Johannesburg, 2014, p. 22.

Finmark Trust, "Terms of Reference: Understanding Other (non SA) SADC Remittance Corridors" 14 June 2016.

Finmark Trust, "Terms of Reference: Cross-Border Remittance Pricing: Understanding the Value Chain and Cost Drivers of Remittance Offerings" 5 July 2016.

J. Fish, "Rights Across Borders: Policies, Protections and Practices for Migrant Domestic Workers in South Africa" In Darcy du Toit, (ed.), *Exploited, Undervalued and Essential: Domestic Workers and the Realisation of Their Rights* (Pretoria, 2013), pp. 213-64.

B. Girdler-Brown et al, "The Burden of Silicosis, Pulmonary Tuberculosis and COPD Among Former Basotho Goldminers" *American Journal of Industrial Medicine* 51(2008).

L. Griffin, "Borderwork: 'Illegality', Unbounded Labour and the Lives of Basotho Migrant Domestic Workers" PhD Thesis, University of Melbourne, 2010.

D. Hammett, "Physician Migration in The Global South Between Cuba and South Africa" *International Migration* 52(2014).

R. Hansen, *An Assessment of Principal Regional Consultative Processes on Migration* (Geneva, 2010).

M. Kiwanuka et al, *Getting the House in Order: Foreign Migrant Workers in the Domestic Work Sector in South Africa* MiWorc Report No. 10, Johannesburg, 2015.

W. Landau and K. Vanyoro, *Adoption of the SADC Labour Migration Policy Framework*. MiWorc Policy Update 1, ACMS Johannesburg, 2015.

D. Lincoln, "Labour migration in the Global Division of Labour: Migrant workers in Mauritius" *International Migration* 47 (2009): 129-156.

D. Lincoln, "Sewing Machinists and Bricklayers Abroad: Migrant Labour and development in Mauritius" *Journal of Mauritian Studies* 1 (2015): 4-27.

G. Mohan and D. Kale, "The Invisible Hand of South-South Globalisation: Chinese Migrants in Africa" Report for the Rockefeller Foundation, Washington DC, 2007.

L. Mpedi and M. Nyenti, *Portability of Social Security Benefits in Mining Sector: Challenges Experienced by Former Mineworkers in Accessing Social Security Benefits in Selected Southern African Countries* (Pretoria: Southern Africa Trust, 2013).

G. Mthembu-Salter et al, *Counting the Cost of Securitising South Africa's Immigration Regime*, Migrating Out of Poverty Working Paper No. 20, University of Sussex, 2014.

J. Munakamwe and Z. Jinnah, *A Bitter Harvest: Migrant Workers in the Commercial Agricultural Sector in South Africa* MiWorc Policy Brief No. 5, Johannesburg, 2015.

C. Nshimbi and L. Fioramonti, *A Region Without Borders? Policy Frameworks for Regional Labour Migration Towards South Africa*. MiWorc Report No. 1, ACMS Johannesburg, 2013.

T. O'Neil et al, *Women on the Move: Migration, Gender Equality and the 2030 Agenda for Sustainable Development* (London: Overseas Development Institute: 2016).

M. Olivier, *Regional Overview of Social Protection for Non-Citizens in the Southern African Development Community*, World Bank, Washington DC, 2009, p. 63.

I. Omelaniuk (ed.), *Global Perspectives on Migration and Development: GFMD Puerto Vallarta and Beyond* (London, 2012).

J. Oucho and J. Crush, "Contra Free Movement: South Africa and the SADC Migration Protocols" *Africa Today* 48(2001): 139-158.

S. Peberdy, "Informal Sector Enterprise and Employment in Gauteng" GCRO Data Brief No. 6, GCRO, Johannesburg, 2015.

S. Peberdy, *International Migrants in Johannesburg's Informal Economy*, SAMP Migration Policy Series No. 71, Cape Town, 2016.

W. Pendleton et al, *Migration, Remittances and Development in Southern Africa*. SAMP Migration Policy Series No. 44, Cape Town, 2006.

H. Postel, "Following the Money: Chinese Labor Migration to Zambia" *Migration Information Source* 20 February 2015.

J. Rademeyer, "Is South Africa the Largest Recipient of Asylum-Seekers Worldwide?" *Africa Check* 11 July 2013.

D. Ratha et al, *Leveraging Migration for Africa: Remittances, Skills and Investments* (Washington DC, 2011).

M. Richter et al, "Migration Status, Work Conditions and Health Utilization of Female Sex Workers in Three South African Cities" *Journal of Immigrant and Minority Health* 16(2014): 7-17.

B. Roberts, *A Migration Audit of Poverty Reduction Strategies in Southern Africa*. MIDSA Report No. 3, SAMP and IOM, 2007, p. 26.

B. Rutherford, "Zimbabweans on the Farms of Northern South Africa" In Crush and Tevera, *Zimbabwe's Exodus*, pp. 244-68.

J. Schachter, *Data Assessment of Labour Migration Statistics in the SADC Region: South Africa, Zambia, Zimbabwe*. Report for IOM Regional Office for Southern Africa, Pretoria, 2009, p. 13.

M. Sefika, *Enhancing Data Migration Management Systems in Lesotho: Assessment and Recommendations*. ACP Migration Observatory Report, Brussels, 2013.

A. Segatti, "Explaining the Impasse of Circular Migration in Southern Africa: From the Migrant Labour System to Deregulation" In C. Solé et al. (eds.), *Impact of Circular Migration on Human, Political and Civil Rights* (London, 2016), pp. 85-108.

A. Segatti and L. Landau (eds.), *Contemporary Migration to South Africa: A Regional Development Issue* (Washington DC, 2011).

Save the Children, *They Say "I'm Lucky I Have a Job": A Participatory Study with Migrant Girls Who Do Domestic Work in Zambia, Zimbabwe and South Africa* (London, 2011).

Solidarity Center, *Domestic Workers and Socio-Economic Rights: A South African Case Study* (Washington DC, 2013).

Solidarity Peace Trust and PASSOP, *Perils and Pitfalls: Migrants and Deportation in South Africa* (Johannesburg, 2012).

Southern Africa Trust, *The Portability and Access of Social Security Benefits for Mine Workers in Southern Africa* Regional Dialogue Report, Johannesburg, 23-25 February 2015.

Southern Hemisphere Consulting, "Fieldwork Report for Harnessing Migration for Inclusive Growth and Development in Southern Africa" Cape Town, 2 July 2016.

Statistics Botswana, *Work Permits Holders, Third Quarter 2012* (Gaborone, 2014).

Statistics South Africa, *Census 2011: Migration Dynamics in South Africa* (Pretoria: Statistics South Africa, 2014).

Statistics South Africa, *Documented Immigrants in South Africa: 2014.* Statistical Release P0351.4, Statistics South Africa (Pretoria, 2015).

Statistics South Africa, *Documented Immigrants in South Africa, 2011, 2012, 2013* (Pretoria: Statistics South Africa, 2012-14).

G. Tawodzera et al, *International Migrants and Refugees in Cape Town's Informal Economy*, SAMP Migration Policy Series No. 70, Cape Town, 2015.

D. Tevera, "10 Years of MIDSA" Ministerial Conference on Managing Migration Through Regional Co-operation, Windhoek, 2010.

D. Tevera and J. Crush, "Discontent and Departure: Attitudes of Skilled Zimbabweans Towards Emigration" In J. Crush and D. Tevera, *Zimbabwe's Exodus*, pp. 112-32.

T. Ulicki and J. Crush, "Poverty, Gender and Migrancy: Lesotho's Migrant Farmworkers in South Africa" In J. Crush and B. Frayne, (eds.), *Surviving on the Move: Migration, Poverty and Development in Southern Africa* (Midrand, 2010), pp. 164-82.

N. Van Hear, *Mixed Migration: Policy Primer* (Oxford, 2011).

M. Visser and S. Ferrer, *Farm Workers' Living and Working Conditions* (Pretoria: ILO, 2015).

Zamstats, *Zambia 2010 Census of Population and Housing: Migration and Urbanisation Analytical Report* (Lusaka, 2013).

ENDNOTES

1 Southern Africa is defined in this report as co-terminous with the countries of the Southern African Development Community (SADC).

2 Jason Schachter, *Data Assessment of Labour Migration Statistics in the SADC Region: South Africa, Zambia, Zimbabwe.* Report for IOM Regional Office for Southern Africa, Pretoria, 2009, p. 13; see also Debbie Budlender, *Improving the Quality of Available Statistics on Foreign Labour in South Africa: Existing Data Sets.* MiWORC Report No. 2, Johannesburg, 2013; M. Sefika, *Enhancing Data Migration Management Systems in Lesotho: Assessment and Recommendations.* ACP Migration Observatory Report, Brussels, 2013.

3 Southern Hemisphere Consulting, "Fieldwork Report for Harnessing Migration for Inclusive Growth and Development in Southern Africa" Cape Town, 2 July 2106.

4 Aurelia Segatti and Loren Landau (eds.), *Contemporary Migration to South Africa: A Regional Development Issue* (Washington DC, 2011).

5 Jonathan Crush and Daniel Tevera (eds.), *Zimbabwe's Exodus: Crisis, Migration, Survival* (Cape Town, 2010).

6 The UNDP figure for 2015 is 3,108,104 based on the rate of increase between 2005 and 2010. However, as it is unlikely that the migrant stock of South Africa has increased by 1.2 million people in the last 5 years (given that there has been a decline in asylum-seeking and a stabilization in migrant flows from Zimbabwe). We have therefore recalculated this figure based on the rate of increase recorded between 2000 and 2010.

7 Interview with Graham Herbert, Managing Director, Teba Ltd, 30 June 2016.

8 Julian Rademeyer, "Is South Africa the Largest Recipient of Asylum-Seekers Worldwide?" *Africa Check* 11 July 2013.

9 Department of Home Affairs, *Green Paper on International Migration in South Africa* (Pretoria, 2016), p. 30.

10 Department of Home Affairs, "2015 Asylum Statistics: Analysis and Trends for the Period January to December" Portfolio Committee on Home Affairs, 23 April 2015.

11 M. Apleni, "An Overview of the New Immigration Laws and Regulations and their Implications" Presentation to Parliamentary Portfolio Committee on Home Affairs, 23 April 2015; Roni Amit, "Paying for Protection:

Corruption in South Africa's Asylum System" *Migration Information Source* 5 November 2015.

12 Nicholas Van Hear, *Mixed Migration: Policy Primer* (Oxford, 2011).

13 Jonathan Crush, Godfrey Tawodzera and Abel Chikanda, "The Third Wave: Mixed Migration from Zimbabwe to South Africa" *Canadian Journal of African Studies* 49(2015): 363-82.

14 Aurelia Segatti, "Explaining the Impasse of Circular Migration in Southern Africa: From the Migrant Labour System to Deregulation" In C. Solé et al. (eds.), *Impact of Circular Migration on Human, Political and Civil Rights* (London, 2016), pp. 85-108.

15 SSA, *Census 2011: Migration Dynamics in South Africa* (Pretoria: Statistics South Africa). Census data from other SADC countries would need to be analyzed to see if this picture holds across the region.

16 Wade Pendleton et al, *Migration, Remittances and Development in Southern Africa*. SAMP Migration Policy Series No. 44, Cape Town, 2006.

17 Solidarity Peace Trust and PASSOP, *Perils and Pitfalls: Migrants and Deportation in South Africa* (Johannesburg, 2012); Gregory Mthembu-Salter et al, *Counting the Cost of Securitising South Africa's Immigration Regime*, Migrating Out of Poverty Working Paper No. 20, University of Sussex, 2014.

18 Interview with Department of Home Affairs Officials, Pretoria.

19 SSA, *Census 2011: Migration Dynamics in South Africa* (Pretoria: Statistics South Africa, 2014).

20 Ibid.

21 Christine Fauvelle-Aymar, *Migration and Employment in South Africa: An Econometric Analysis of Domestic and International Migrants*, MiWorc Report No. 6, ACMS Johannesburg, 2014, p. 22.

22 Debbie Budlender, *Improving the Quality of Available Statistics on Foreign Labour in South Africa: Existing Data-Sets*. MiWorc Report No 2, ACMS Johannesburg, 2013.

23 Fauvelle-Aymar, *Migration and Employment in South Africa*.

24 Zamstats, *Zambia 2010 Census of Population and Housing: Migration and Urbanisation Analytical Report* (Lusaka, 2013).

25 Hannah Postel, "Following the Money: Chinese Labor Migration to Zambia" *Migration Information Source* 20 February 2015.

26 SSA, *Documented Immigrants in South Africa: 2014*. Statistical Release P0351.4, Statistics South Africa, Pretoria, 2015

27 SSA, *Documented Immigrants in South Africa, 2011, 2012, 2013* (Pretoria: Statistics South Africa, 2012-14).

28 Postel, "Following the Money."

29 Daniel Tevera and Jonathan Crush, "Discontent and Departure: Attitudes of Skilled Zimbabweans Towards Emigration" In Crush and Tevera, *Zimbabwe's Exodus*, pp. 112-32; Jonathan Crush and Wade Pendleton, "Brain Flight: The Exodus of Health Professionals from South Africa" *International Journal of International Migration, Health and Social Care* 6(2010): 3-18; Jonathan Crush and Wade Pendleton, "The Brain Drain Potential of Students in the African Health and Nonhealth Sectors" *International Journal of Population Research* 2012 ArticleID274305; doi:10.1155/2012/274305.

30 Irena Omelaniuk (ed.), *Global Perspectives on Migration and Development: GFMD Puerto Vallarta and Beyond* (London, 2012).

31 Belinda Dodson, "Gender, Migration and Livelihoods: Migrant Women in Southern Africa" In N. Piper (Ed.), *New Perspectives on Gender and Migration* (London, 2013).

32 Ibid.

33 Steffen Angenendt, *Triple-Win Migration: Challenges and Opportunities*. Migration Strategy Group, German Marshall Fund of US, 2014.

34 Daniel Hammett, "Physician Migration in The Global South Between Cuba and South Africa" *International Migration* 52 (2014).

35 David Lincoln, "Labour migration in the Global Division of Labour: Migrant workers in Mauritius" *International Migration* 47 (2009): 129-156.

36 Giles Mohan and Dinar Kale, "The Invisible Hand of South-South Globalisation: Chinese Migrants in Africa" Report for the Rockefeller Foundation, Washington DC, 2007.

37 David Lincoln, "Sewing Machinists and Bricklayers Abroad: Migrant Labour and Development in Mauritius" *Journal of Mauritian Studies* 1 (2015): 4-27.

38 Natalia Dinat and Sally Peberdy, *Migrants in Domestic Work in South Africa*. SAMP Migration Policy Series No. 40, Johannesburg, 2005; Debbie Budlender, "Decent Work for Domestic Workers" Study for Services Sector Education and Training Sector, CASE, Johannesburg, 2010; Laura Griffin, "Borderwork: "Illegality", Unbounded Labour and the Lives of Basotho Migrant Domestic Workers" PhD Thesis, University of Melbourne, 2010; Jennifer Fish, "Rights Across Borders: Policies, Protections and Practices for Migrant Domestic Workers in South Africa" In Darcy du Toit, ed., *Exploited, Undervalued and Essential: Domestic Workers and the Realisation of Their Rights* (Pretoria, 2013), pp. 213-64; Solidarity Center, *Domestic Workers and Socio-Economic Rights: A South African Case Study*. Washington DC, 2013; M. Kiwanuka et al, *Getting the House in Order: Foreign Migrant Workers in the Domestic Work Sector in South Africa,* MiWorc Report No. 10, Johannesburg, 2015.

39 Blair Rutherford, "Zimbabweans on the Farms of Northern South Africa" In Crush and Tevera, *Zimbabwe's Exodus*, pp. 244-68; Teresa Ulicki and Jonathan Crush, "Poverty, Gender and Migrancy: Lesotho's Migrant Farmworkers in South Africa" In Jonathan Crush and Bruce Frayne, eds., *Surviving on the Move* (Midrand, 2010), pp. 164-82; Janet Munakamwe and Zaheera Jinnah, *A Bitter Harvest: Migrant Workers in the Commercial Agricultural Sector in South Africa* MiWorc Policy Brief No. 5, Johannesburg, 2015; Margareet Visser and Stuart Ferrer, *Farm Workers' Living and Working Conditions* (Pretoria: ILO, 2015).

40 Jonathan Crush, Abel Chikanda and Caroline Skinner, eds., *Mean Streets: Migration, Xenophobia and Informality in South Africa* (Ottawa and Cape Town, 2015).

41 Marlise Richter et al "Migration Status, Work Conditions and Health Utilization of Female Sex Workers in Three South African Cities" *Journal of Immigrant and Minority Health* 16(2014): 7-17.

42 Kiwanuka et al, *Getting the House in Order.*

43 Save the Children, *They Say "I'm Lucky I Have a Job": A Participatory Study with Migrant Girls Who Do Domestic Work in Zambia, Zimbabwe and South Africa* (London, 2011).

44 Marius Oliveer, *Regional Overview of Social Protection for Non-Citizens in the Southern African Development Community*, World Bank, Washington DC, 2009, p. 63.

45 Bob Deacon, Marius Olivier and Reason Beremauro, *Social Security and Social Protection of Migrants in South Africa and SADC*, MiWorc Report No. 8, Johannesburg, 2013.

46 The challenge of securing these payments for ex-miners was the subject of Southern Africa Trust workshops in February 2014 and March 2015; see L. Mpedi and M. Nyenti, *Portability of Social Security Benefits in Mining Sector: Challenges Experienced by Former Mineworkers in Accessing Social Security Benefits in Selected Southern African Countries* (Pretoria: Southern Africa Trust, 2013); Southern Africa Trust, *The Portability and Access of Social Security Benefits for Mine Workers in Southern Africa* Regional Dialogue Report, Johannesburg, 23-25 February 2015.

47 B. Girdler-Brown et al, "The Burden of Silicosis, Pulmonary Tuberculosis and COPD Among Former Basotho Goldminers" *American Journal of Industrial Medicine* 51(2008); R. Ehrlich, "A Century of Miners' Compensation in South Africa" *American Journal of Industrial Medicine* 55(2012).

48 In March 2016, Anglo American and AngloGold Ashanti reached a ZAR460 million settlement with 4,400 gold miners, an indication of the sums likely to be involved in the class-action lawsuit.

49 DNA Economics, *Remittance Channel*, p. iv.

50 FinMark Trust is conducting several studies on remittance corridors; see "Terms of Reference: Understanding Other (non-SA) SADC Remittance Corridors" 14 June 2016; "Terms of Reference: Cross-Border Remittance Pricing: Understanding the Value Chain and Cost Drivers of Remittance Offerings" 5 July 2016; and the pilot project "Shoprite Money Transfers Lesotho."

51 Ibid.

52 Jonathan Crush and Mary Caesar, *Food Remittances: Migration and Food Security in Africa*, SAMP Migration Policy Series No. 72, Cape Town, 2016.

53 UN-INSTRAW, *Development and Migration from a Gender Perspective*; IOM, *Gender, Migration and Remittances.*

54 Sally Peberdy, "Informal Sector Enterprise and Employment in Gauteng" GCRO Data Brief No. 6, GCRO, Johannesburg, 2015.

55 Fauvelle-Aymar, *Migration and Employment in South Africa*, p. 25.

56 Godfrey Tawodzera et al, *International Migrants and Refugees in Cape Town's Informal Economy*, SAMP Migration Policy Series No. 70, Cape Town, 2015; Sally Peberdy, *International Migrants in Johannesburg's Informal Economy*, SAMP Migration Policy Series No. 71, Cape Town, 2016.

57 Ibid.

58 Diaspora Liaison Office and IOM Zambia, *Zambian Diaspora Survey – Report Feeding into the Development of a Diaspora Engagement Framework for Zambia* (Lusaka, 2011); Diaspora Liaison Office and IOM Zambia, "Updated Summary Report of the Zambian Diaspora Survey" Lusaka, 2014.

59 Jonathan Crush et al, *Divided Diasporas: Southern Africans in Canada* (Waterloo, 2013).

60 Sujata Ramachandran, "Benevolent Funds: Philanthropic Practices of the South African Diaspora in Ontario, Canada" In Abel Chikanda, Jonathan Crush and Margaret Walton-Roberts (eds.), *Diasporas, Development and Governance* (London, 2016), pp. 65-82.

61 See Global Forum on Migration and Development at http://www.gfmd.org/; http://www.un.org/en/ga/68/meetings/migration/; UN High Level Dialogue on Migration and Development at http://www.un.org/en/ga/68/meetings/migration/; Diaspora Ministerial Conference at http://www.iom.int/files/live/sites/iom/files/What-We-Do/idm/workshops/IDM-2013-Diaspora-Ministerial-Conference/DMC_Final_Conference_Report.pdf and Migration Dialogue for Southern Africa (MIDSA) at https://www.iom.int/midsa

62 Benjamin Roberts, *A Migration Audit of Poverty Reduction Strategies in Southern Africa*, MIDSA Report No. 3, SAMP and IOM, 2007, p. 26; see *http://www.sadc.int/about-sadc/overview/strategic-pl/regional-indicative-strategic-development-plan/*

63 John Oucho and Jonathan Crush, "Contra Free Movement: South Africa and the SADC Migration Protocols" *Africa Today* 48(2001): 139-158.

64 Christopher Nshimbi and Lorenzo Fioramonti, *A Region Without Borders? Policy Frameworks for Regional Labour Migration Towards South Africa*, MiWorc Report No. 1, ACMS Johannesburg, 2013, p. 83

65 Ibid., pp. 64-74.

66 Roberts, *Migration Audit of Poverty Reduction Strategies*, p. 79.

67 Nshimbi and Fioramonti, *Region Without Borders?*, p. 107.

68 Jonathan Crush, "Towards the Triple Win: Lower-Skilled Labour Migration to South Africa" Paper for Colloquium on a New International Migration Policy Paradigm for South Africa, Department of Home Affairs, 2015.

69 Belinda Dodson and Jonathan Crush, *Migration Governance and Migrant Rights in the Southern African Development Community (SADC)*. UNRISD Research Paper 2015-3, Geneva, 2015.

70 P. de Guchteneire et al, *Migration and Human Rights: The United Nations Convention on Migrant Workers' Rights* (Cambridge and Paris, 2009), pp. 247-77.

71 See http://www.satucc.org/sadc-protocol-on-employment-labour/

72 Wendy Landau and Kuda Vanyoro, *Adoption of the SADC Labour Migration Policy Framework*, MiWorc Policy Update 1, ACMS Johannesburg, 2015.

73 See http://www.ilo.org/addisababa/areas-of-work/labour-migration/WCMS_379400/lang--en/index.htm

74 African Development Bank, *African Development Report 2014: Regional Integration for Inclusive Growth* (Abidjan, 2014).

75 Tam O'Neil et al, *Women on the Move: Migration, Gender Equality and the 2030 Agenda for Sustainable Development* (London: Overseas Development Institute, 2016).

76 Daniel Tevera and Jonathan Crush, "10 Years of MIDSA" Ministerial Conference on Managing Migration Through Regional Cooperation, Windhoek, 2010.

77 R. Hansen, *An Assessment of Principal Regional Consultative Processes on Migration* (Geneva, 2010).

78 See https://www.iom.int/midsa

79 See http://www.iom.int/files/live/sites/iom/files/What-We-Do/docs/15-17-November-2010-Windhoek-Namibia-MIDSA-Ministerial-Conference-on-Migration-through-Regional-Cooperation.pdf

80 Interview with Dr Josiah Ogina, IOM Regional Office, Pretoria.

81 Tam O'Neil, Anjali Fleury and Marta Foresti, "Women on the Move: Migration, Gender Equality and the 2030 Agenda for Sustainable Development" Overseas Development Institute, London, 2016; UN-INSTRAW and UNDP, *Migration, Remittances and Gender-Responsive Local Development* (New York, 2010).

82 Ibid., p. 28.

83 Sonia Plaza, Mario Navarrete and Dilip Ratha, *Migration and Remittances Household Surveys: Methodological Issues and New Findings from Sub-Saharan Africa* (Washington DC: World Bank 2011); Dilip Ratha, Sanket Mohapatra, Caglar Ozden, Sonia Plaza, William Shaw, and Abebe Shimeles, *Leveraging Migration for Africa: Remittances, Skills*

and Investments (Washington DC: World Bank, 2011). With the exception of South Africa (whose apparently problematic data has never been released), there were no SADC countries in the Project. There has seemingly been no systematic gender analysis of the data either: http://microdata.worldbank.org/index.php/catalog/mrs

84 See the following SAMP Reports: No. 43: *Migration and Development in Mozambique: Poverty, Inequality and Survival* (Cape Town, 2006); No 44: *Migration, Remittances and Development in Southern Africa* (Cape Town, 2006); No 49: *Gender, Migration and Remittances in Southern Africa* (Cape Town, 2008); No. 52: *Migration, Remittances and 'Development' in Lesotho* (Cape Town, 2010).

85 Domestic Workers Convention, 2011 (No, 189).

86 Jonathan Crush and Wade Pendleton, "Remitting for Survival: Rethinking the Development Potential of Remittances in Southern Africa" *Global Development Studies* 5(3/4) (2009): 53-84; Bruce Frayne and Wade Pendleton, "The Development Role of Remittances in the Urbanization Process in Southern Africa" *Global Development Studies* 5(3/4) (2009): 86-132.

87 DNA Economics, *The South Africa-SADC Remittance Channel*. Report for FinMark Trust, February 2012

88 Belinda Dodson, *Gender, Migration and Remittances in Southern Africa*, SAMP Migration Policy Series No. 49, Cape Town, 2008.

89 Ratha et al, *Leveraging Migration for Africa: Remittances, Skills and Investments*.

90 IFAD, *2016 Call for Proposals: Scaling Up Remittances (SURE)* at https://www.ifad.org/documents/10180/44a97ad4-aae9-4e6b-b89f-81265a5c434b

91 http://www.state.gov/p/af/rt/awep/

92 http://www.ilo.org/empent/areas/womens-entrepreneur-ship-development-wed/lang--en/index.htm

93 Chukwe-Emeka Chikezie, "Reinforcing the Contributions of African Diasporas to Development" In S. Plaza and D. Ratha, eds., *Diaspora for Development in Africa* (Washington DC, 2011), pp. 261-82.

94 Ibid.

95 Ibid., p. 279.

96 Christian Kingombe, "A Diaspora for Development? The Role of DRC's Diaspora in the Country's Future" Overseas Development Institute 8 December 2011.

97 Lulessa Abadura, Brigitte Fahrenhorst and Frank Zelazny, "Untapped Potential: Engaging Basotho Diasporas in the South for National Development" ACP Migration Observatory Report, Brussels, 2014.

98 Jonathan Crush and Abel Chikanda, "Diaspora Engagement Policies in National Context: South Africa" In Jack Mangala, ed., *Africa and its Global Diaspora: The Policy and Politics of Emigration* (London, 2016).

99 Harold Utouh and Darlene Mutalemwa, "Engaging the Tanzanian Diaspora in National Development: What Do We Know and What Are the Gaps" *African Journal of Economic Review* 3(2015).

100 Diaspora Liaison Office (DLO) and IOM, *Diaspora Engagement and Mobilization Framework for Zambia* (Lusaka, 2011).